MACBETH

WILLIAM SHAKESPEARE

෨෫෪

CONTENTS

DRAMATIS PERSONÆ

Duncan, king of Scotland.
Malcolm,
Donalbain,
Macbeth,
Banquo,
Macduff,
Lennox,
Ross,
Menteith,
Angus,
Caithness,
Fleance, son to Banquo.
Siward, earl of Northumberland, general of
    the English forces.
Young Siward, his son.
Seyton, an officer attending on Macbeth.
Boy, son to Macduff.
An English Doctor.
A Scotch Doctor.
A Sergeant.
A Porter.
An Old Man.
Lady Macbeth.

Lady Macduff.
Gentlewoman attending on Lady Macbeth.
Hecate.
Three Witches.
Apparitions.
Lords, Gentlemen, Officers, Soldiers,
    Murderers, Attendants, and Messengers

Scene: Scotland: England.

ACT I.

SCENE I. A DESERT PLACE.

(Thunder and lightning. Enter three Witches.)

FIRST WITCH. When shall we three meet
    again
In thunder, lightning, or in rain?
SEC. WITCH. When the hurlyburly's done,
When the battle's lost and won.
THIRD WITCH. That will be ere the set of
    sun. ₅
FIRST WITCH. Where the place?
SEC. WITCH. Upon the heath.
THIRD WITCH. There to meet with Macbeth.
FIRST WITCH. I come, Graymalkin.
ALL. Paddock calls:—anon!
Fair is foul, and foul is fair. ₁₀
Hover through the fog and filthy air. *(Exeunt.)*

SCENE II. A CAMP NEAR FORRES

(Alarum within. Enter Duncan, Malcolm, Donalbain, Lennox, with Attendants, meeting a bleeding Sergeant.)

DUN. What bloody man is that? He can report,
As seemeth by his plight, of the revolt
The newest state.
MAL. This is the sergeant
Who like a good and hardy soldier fought
'Gainst my captivity. Hail, brave friend! 5
Say to the king the knowledge of the broil
As thou didst leave it.
SER. Doubtful it stood;
As two spent swimmers, that do cling together
And choke their art. The merciless Macdonwald—
Worthy to be a rebel, for to that 10
The multiplying villanies of nature
Do swarm upon him—from the western isles
Of kerns and gallowglasses is supplied;
And fortune, on his damned quarrel smiling,
Show'd like a rebel's whore: but all's too weak: 15
For brave Macbeth—well he deserves that name—
Disdaining fortune, with his brandish'd steel,
Which smoked with bloody execution,
Like valour's minion carved out his passage
Till he faced the slave; 20
Which ne'er shook hands, nor bade farewell to him,
Till he unseam'd him from the nave to the chaps,
And fix'd his head upon our battlements.
DUN. O valiant cousin! worthy gentleman!

SER. As whence the sun 'gins his reflection $_{25}$
Shipwrecking storms and direful thunders
  break,
So from that spring whence comfort seem'd
  to come
Discomfort swells. Mark, king of Scotland,
  mark:
No sooner justice had, with valour arm'd,
Compell'd these skipping kerns to trust their
  heels, $_{30}$
But the Norweyan lord, surveying vantage,
With furbish'd arms and new supplies of men,
Began a fresh assault.
DUN. Dismay'd not this
Our captains, Macbeth and Banquo?
SER. Yes;
As sparrows eagles, or the hare the lion. $_{35}$
If I say sooth, I must report they were
As cannons overcharged with double cracks;
So they
Doubly redoubled strokes upon the foe:
Except they meant to bathe in reeking
  wounds, $_{40}$
Or memorize another Golgotha,
I cannot tell—
But I am faint; my gashes cry for help.
DUN. So well thy words become thee as thy
  wounds;
They smack of honour both. Go get him
  surgeons. $_{45}$

(Exit Sergeant, attended.)

Who comes here?

(Enter Ross.)

MAL. The worthy thane of Ross.

LEN. What a haste looks through his eyes! So
    should he look

That seems to speak things strange.

ROSS. God save the king!

DUN. Whence camest thou, worthy thane?

ROSS. From Fife, great king;

Where the Norweyan banners flout the sky 50

And fan our people cold.

Norway himself, with terrible numbers,

Assisted by that most disloyal traitor

The thane of Cawdor, began a dismal
    conflict;

Till that Bellona's bridegroom, lapp'd in
    proof, 55

Confronted him with self-comparisons,

Point against point rebellious, arm
    'gainst arm,

Curbing his lavish spirit: and, to conclude,

The victory fell on us.

DUN. Great happiness!

ROSS. That now 60

Sweno, the Norways' king, craves composition;

Nor would we deign him burial of his men

Till he disbursed, at Saint Colme's inch,

Ten thousand dollars to our general use.

DUN. No more that thane of Cawdor shall
    deceive 65

Our bosom interest: go pronounce his present
    death,

And with his former title greet Macbeth.

ROSS. I'll see it done.

DUN. What he hath lost, noble Macbeth
    hath won.

(Exeunt.)

SCENE III. A HEATH.

(Thunder. Enter the three Witches.)

FIRST WITCH. Where hast thou been, sister?
SEC. WITCH. Killing swine.
THIRD WITCH. Sister, where thou?
FIRST WITCH. A sailor's wife had chestnuts
    in her lap,
And mounch'd, and mounch'd, and
    mounch'd. 'Give me,' quoth I: 5
'Aroint thee, witch!' the rump-fed ronyon
    cries.
Her husband's to Aleppo gone, master o' the
    Tiger:
But in a sieve I'll thither sail,
And, like a rat without a tail,
I'll do, I'll do, and I'll do. 10
SEC. WITCH. I'll give thee a wind.
FIRST WITCH. Thou'rt kind.
THIRD WITCH. And I another.
FIRST WITCH. I myself have all the other;
And the very ports they blow, 15
All the quarters that they know
I' the shipman's card.
I will drain him dry as hay:
Sleep shall neither night nor day
Hang upon his pent-house lid; 20
He shall live a man forbid:
Weary se'nnights nine times nine
Shall he dwindle, peak, and pine:
Though his bark cannot be lost,
Yet it shall be tempest-tost. 25
Look what I have.
SEC. WITCH. Show me, show me.
FIRST WITCH. Here I have a pilot's thumb,

Wreck'd as homeward he did come. *(Drum within.)*

THIRD WITCH. A drum, a drum! [30]
Macbeth doth come.

ALL. The weird sisters, hand in hand,
Posters of the sea and land,
Thus do go about, about:
Thrice to thine, and thrice to mine, [35]
And thrice again, to make up nine.
Peace! the charm's wound up.

(Enter Macbeth and Banquo.)

MACB. So foul and fair a day I have not seen.
BAN. How far is't call'd to Forres? What are these
So wither'd, and so wild in their attire, [40]
That look not like the inhabitants o' the earth,
And yet are on't? Live you? or are you aught
That man may question? You seem to understand me,
By each at once her choppy finger laying
Upon her skinny lips: you should be women, [45]
And yet your beards forbid me to interpret
That you are so.
MACB. Speak, if you can: what are you?
FIRST WITCH. All hail, Macbeth! hail to thee, thane of Glamis!
SEC. WITCH. All hail, Macbeth! hail to thee, thane of Cawdor!
THIRD WITCH. All hail, Macbeth, that shalt be king hereafter![50]
BAN. Good sir, why do you start, and seem to fear

Things that do sound so fair? I' the name of
    truth,
Are ye fantastical, or that indeed
Which outwardly ye show? My noble partner
You greet with present grace and great
    prediction 55
Of noble having and of royal hope,
That he seems rapt withal: to me you
    speak not:
If you can look into the seeds of time,
And say which grain will grow and which
    will not,
Speak then to me, who neither beg nor fear 60
Your favours nor your hate.
FIRST WITCH. *Hail!*
SEC. WITCH. *Hail!*
THIRD WITCH. *Hail!*
FIRST WITCH. Lesser than Macbeth, and
    greater. 65
SEC. WITCH. Not so happy, yet much
    happier.
THIRD WITCH. Thou shalt get kings, though
    thou be none:
So all hail, Macbeth and Banquo!
FIRST WITCH. Banquo and Macbeth, all
    hail!
MACB. Stay, you imperfect speakers, tell me
    more: 70
By Sinel's death I know I am thane of
    Glamis;
But how of Cawdor? the thane of Cawdor
    lives,
A prosperous gentleman; and to be king
Stands not within the prospect of belief,
No more than to be Cawdor. Say from
    whence 75
You owe this strange intelligence? or why

9

Upon this blasted heath you stop our way
With such prophetic greeting? Speak, I
   charge you.

(Witches vanish.)

BAN. The earth hath bubbles as the
   water has,
And these are of them: whither are they
   vanish'd? 80
MACB. Into the air, and what seem'd
   corporal melted
As breath into the wind. Would they had
   stay'd!
BAN. Were such things here as we do speak
   about?
Or have we eaten on the insane root
That takes the reason prisoner? 85
MACB. Your children shall be kings.
BAN. You shall be king.
MACB. And thane of Cawdor too: went it
   not so?
BAN. To the selfsame tune and words. Who's
   here?

(Enter Ross and Angus.)

ROSS. The king hath happily received,
   Macbeth,
The news of thy success: and when he
   reads 90
Thy personal venture in the rebels' fight,
His wonders and his praises do contend
Which should be thine or his: silenced with
   that,
In viewing o'er the rest o' the selfsame day,
He finds thee in the stout Norweyan ranks, 95

Nothing afeard of what thyself didst make,
Strange images of death. As thick as hail
Came post with post, and every one did bear
Thy praises in his kingdom's great defence,
And pour'd them down before him.

ANG. We are sent ₁₀₀
To give thee, from our royal master, thanks;
Only to herald thee into his sight,
Not pay thee.

ROSS. And for an earnest of a greater
honour,
He bade me, from him, call thee thane of
Cawdor: ₁₀₅
In which addition, hail, most worthy thane!
For it is thine.

BAN. What, can the devil speak true?

MACB. The thane of Cawdor lives: why do
you dress me
In borrow'd robes?

ANG. Who was the thane lives yet,
But under heavy judgement bears that life ₁₁₀
Which he deserves to lose. Whether he was
combined
With those of Norway, or did line the rebel
With hidden help and vantage, or that
with both
He labour'd in his country's wreck, I
know not;
But treasons capital, confess'd and proved, ₁₁₅
Have overthrown him.

MACB. *(Aside)* Glamis, and thane of Cawdor:
The greatest is behind.—Thanks for your
pains.—
Do you not hope your children shall be kings,
When those that gave the thane of Cawdor
to me
Promised no less to them?

BAN. That, trusted home, 120
Might yet enkindle you unto the crown,
Besides the thane of Cawdor. But 'tis strange:
And oftentimes, to win us to our harm,
The instruments of darkness tell us truths,
Win us with honest trifles, to betray 's 125
In deepest consequence.
Cousins, a word, I pray you.
MACB. *(Aside)* Two truths are told,
As happy prologues to the swelling act
Of the imperial theme.—I thank you,
    gentlemen.
(Aside) This supernatural soliciting 130
Cannot be ill; cannot be good: if ill,
Why hath it given me earnest of success,
Commencing in a truth? I am thane of
    Cawdor:
If good, why do I yield to that suggestion
Whose horrid image doth unfix my hair 135
And make my seated heart knock at my ribs,
Against the use of nature? Present fears
Are less than horrible imaginings:
My thought, whose murder yet is but
    fantastical,
Shakes so my single state of man that
    function 140
Is smother'd in surmise, and nothing is
But what is not.
BAN. Look, how our partner's rapt.
MACB. *(Aside)* If chance will have me king,
    why, chance may crown me,
Without my stir.
BAN. New honours come upon him,
Like our strange garments, cleave not to their
    mould 145
But with the aid of use.
MACB. *(Aside)* Come what come may,

Time and the hour runs through the roughest
    day.
BAN. Worthy Macbeth, we stay upon your
    leisure.
MACB. Give me your favour: my dull brain
    was wrought
With things forgotten. Kind gentlemen, your
    pains 150
Are register'd where every day I turn
The leaf to read them. Let us toward the
    king.
Think upon what hath chanced, and at more
    time,
The interim having weigh'd it, let us speak
Our free hearts each to other.
BAN. Very gladly. 155
MACB. Till then, enough. Come, friends.
    (Exeunt.)

SCENE IV. FORRES. THE PALACE

*(Flourish. Enter Duncan, Malcolm, Donalbain, Lennox, and
Attendants.)*

DUN. Is execution done on Cawdor? Are not
Those in commission yet return'd?
MAL. My liege,
They are not yet come back. But I have spoke
With one that saw him die, who did report
That very frankly he confess'd his treasons, 5
Implored your highness' pardon and set forth
A deep repentance: nothing in his life
Became him like the leaving it; he died
As one that had been studied in his death,
To throw away the dearest thing he owed 10
As 'twere a careless trifle.
DUN. There's no art

To find the mind's construction in the face:
He was a gentleman on whom I built
An absolute trust.
(Enter Macbeth, Banquo, Ross, and Angus.)
O worthiest cousin!
The sin of my ingratitude even now ₁₅
Was heavy on me: thou art so far before
That swiftest wing of recompense is slow
To overtake thee. Would thou hadst less
    deserved,
That the proportion both of thanks and
    payment
Might have been mine! only I have left to
    say, ₂₀
More is thy due than more than all can pay.
MACB. The service and the loyalty I owe,
In doing it, pays itself. Your highness' part
Is to receive our duties: and our duties
Are to your throne and state, children and
    servants; ₂₅
Which do but what they should, by doing
    every thing
Safe toward your love and honour.
DUN. Welcome hither:
I have begun to plant thee, and will labour
To make thee full of growing. Noble Banquo,
That hast no less deserved, nor must be
    known ₃₀
No less to have done so: let me infold thee
And hold thee to my heart.
BAN. There if I grow,
The harvest is your own.
DUN. My plenteous joys,
Wanton in fulness, seek to hide themselves
In drops of sorrow. Sons, kinsmen, thanes, ₃₅
And you whose places are the nearest, know,
We will establish our estate upon

Our eldest, Malcolm, whom we name
    hereafter
The Prince of Cumberland: which
    honour must
Not unaccompanied invest him only, 40
But signs of nobleness, like stars, shall shine
On all deservers. From hence to Inverness,
And bind us further to you.

Macb. The rest is labour, which is not used
    for you:
I'll be myself the harbinger, and make
    joyful 45
The hearing of my wife with your approach;
So humbly take my leave.

Dun. My worthy Cawdor!

Macb. *(Aside)* The Prince of Cumberland!
    that is a step,
On which I must fall down, or else o'erleap,
For in my way it lies. Stars, hide your fires; 50
Let not light see my black and deep desires:
The eye wink at the hand; yet let that be
Which the eye fears, when it is done, to see.
    (Exit.)

Dun. True, worthy Banquo; he is full so
    valiant,
And in his commendations I am fed; 55
It is a banquet to me. Let's after him,
Whose care is gone before to bid us
    welcome:
It is a peerless kinsman. *(Flourish. Exeunt.)*

SCENE V. INVERNESS. MACBETH'S
CASTLE: (ENTER LADY MACBETH,
READING A LETTER.)

    Lady M. 'They met me in the day of success;
        and I

have learned by the perfectest report, they
    have more in
them than mortal knowledge. When I burned
    in desire to
question them further, they made themselves
    air, into which
they vanished. Whiles I stood rapt in the
    wonder of it, 5
came missives from the king, who all-hailed
    me "Thane
of Cawdor;" by which title, before, these
    weird sisters saluted
me, and referred me to the coming on of
    time, with
"Hail, king that shalt be!" This have I
    thought good to
deliver thee, my dearest partner of greatness,
    that thou 10
mightst not lose the dues of rejoicing, by
    being ignorant
of what greatness is promised thee. Lay it to
    thy heart,
and farewell.'
Glamis thou art, and Cawdor, and shalt be
What thou art promised: yet do I fear thy
    nature; 15
It is too full o' the milk of human kindness
To catch the nearest way: thou wouldst be
    great;
Art not without ambition, but without
The illness should attend it: what thou
    wouldst highly,
That wouldst thou holily; wouldst not play
    false, 20
And yet wouldst wrongly win: thou'ldst have,
    great Glamis,

That which cries 'Thus thou must do, if thou
    have it;
And that which rather thou dost fear to do
Than wishest should be undone.' Hie thee
    hither,
That I may pour my spirits in thine ear, $_{25}$
And chastise with the valour of my tongue
All that impedes thee from the golden round,
Which fate and metaphysical aid doth seem
To have thee crown'd withal.

(Enter a Messenger.)

What is your tidings?
MESS. The king comes here to-night.
LADY M. Thou'rt mad to say it:$_{30}$
Is not thy master with him? who, were't so,
Would have inform'd for preparation.
MESS. So please you, it is true: our thane is
    coming:
One of my fellows had the speed of him,
Who, almost dead for breath, had scarcely
    more $_{35}$
Than would make up his message.
LADY M. Give him tending;
He brings great news. *(Exit Messenger.)*
The raven himself is hoarse
That croaks the fatal entrance of Duncan
Under my battlements. Come, you spirits
That tend on mortal thoughts, unsex me
    here, $_{40}$
And fill me, from the crown to the toe,
    top-full
Of direst cruelty! make thick my blood,
Stop up the access and passage to remorse,
That no compunctious visitings of nature

Shake my fell purpose, nor keep peace
    between 45
The effect and it! Come to my woman's
    breasts,
And take my milk for gall, you murdering
    ministers,
Wherever in your sightless substances
You wait on nature's mischief! Come, thick
    night,
And pall thee in the dunnest smoke of hell, 50
That my keen knife see not the wound it
    makes,
Nor heaven peep through the blanket of the
    dark,
To cry 'Hold, hold!'
(Enter Macbeth.)
Great Glamis! worthy Cawdor!
Greater than both, by the all-hail hereafter!
Thy letters have transported me beyond 55
This ignorant present, and I feel now
The future in the instant.
MACB. My dearest love,
Duncan comes here to-night.
LADY M. And when goes hence?
MACB. To-morrow, as he purposes.
LADY M. O, never
Shall sun that morrow see! 60
Your face, my thane, is as a book where men
May read strange matters. To beguile the
    time,
Look like the time; bear welcome in your eye,
Your hand, your tongue: look like the
    innocent flower,
But be the serpent under't. He that's
    coming 65
Must be provided for: and you shall put
This night's great business into my dispatch;

Which shall to all our nights and days
    to come
Give solely sovereign sway and masterdom.
Macb. We will speak further.
Lady Macb. Only look up clear; 70
To alter favour ever is to fear:
Leave all the rest to me. *(Exeunt.)*

SCENE VI. BEFORE MACBETH'S CASTLE

*(Hautboys and torches. Enter Duncan, Malcolm, Donalbain,
Banquo, Lennox, Macduff, Ross, Angus, and Attendants.)*

Dun. This castle hath a pleasant seat; the air
Nimbly and sweetly recommends itself
Unto our gentle senses.
Ban. This guest of summer,
The temple-haunting martlet, does approve
By his loved mansionry that the heaven's
    breath 5
Smells wooingly here: no jutty, frieze,
Buttress, nor coign of vantage, but this bird
Hath made his pendent bed and procreant
    cradle:
Where they most breed and haunt, I have
    observed
The air is delicate.

(Enter Lady Macbeth.)

Dun. See, see, our honour'd hostess! 10
The love that follows us sometime is our
    trouble,
Which still we thank as love. Herein I
    teach you
How you shall bid God'ild us for your pains,
And thank us for your trouble.

LADY M. All our service
In every point twice done, and then done
    double, 15
Were poor and single business to contend
Against those honours deep and broad
    wherewith
Your majesty loads our house: for those
    of old,
And the late dignities heap'd up to them,
We rest your hermits.
DUN. Where's the thane of Cawdor? 20
We coursed him at the heels, and had a
    purpose
To be his purveyor: but he rides well,
And his great love, sharp as his spur, hath
    holp him
To his home before us. Fair and noble hostess,
We are your guest to-night.
LADY M. Your servants ever 25
Have theirs, themselves, and what is theirs, in
    compt,
To make their audit at your highness'
    pleasure,
Still to return your own.
DUN. Give me your hand;
Conduct me to mine host: we love him
    highly,
And shall continue our graces towards him. 30
By your leave, hostess. *(Exeunt.)*

SCENE VII. MACBETH'S CASTLE

(Hautboys and torches. Enter a Sewer, and divers Servants with dishes and service and pass over the stage. Then enter Macbeth.)

Macb. If it were done when 'tis done, then
    'twere well
It were done quickly: if the assassination
Could trammel up the consequence, and
    catch,
With his surcease, success; that but this blow
Might be the be-all and the end-all here, 5
But here, upon this bank and shoal of time,
We'ld jump the life to come. But in these
    cases
We still have judgement here; that we but
    teach
Bloody instructions, which being taught
    return
To plague the inventor: this even-handed
    justice 10
Commends the ingredients of our poison'd
    chalice
To our own lips. He's here in double trust:
First, as I am his kinsman and his subject,
Strong both against the deed; then, as his
    host,
Who should against his murderer shut the
    door, 15
Not bear the knife myself. Besides, this
    Duncan
Hath borne his faculties so meek, hath been
So clear in his great office, that his virtues
Will plead like angels trumpet-tongued
    against
The deep damnation of his taking-off; 20
And pity, like a naked new-born babe,
Striding the blast, or heaven's cherubin
    horsed
Upon the sightless couriers of the air,
Shall blow the horrid deed in every eye,

That tears shall drown the wind. I have no
    spur 25
To prick the sides of my intent, but only
Vaulting ambition, which o'erleaps itself
And falls on the other.

(Enter Lady Macbeth.)

How now! what news?
LADY M. He has almost supp'd: why have
    you left the chamber?
MACB. Hath he ask'd for me?
LADY M. Know you not he has? 30
MACB. We will proceed no further in this
    business:
He hath honour'd me of late; and I have
    bought
Golden opinions from all sorts of people,
Which would be worn now in their newest
    gloss,
Not cast aside so soon.
LADY M. Was the hope drunk 35
Wherein you dress'd yourself? hath it slept
    since?
And wakes it now, to look so green and pale
At what it did so freely? From this time
Such I account thy love. Art thou afeard
To be the same in thine own act and valour 40
As thou art in desire? Wouldst thou have that
Which thou esteem'st the ornament of life,
And live a coward in thine own esteem,
Letting 'I dare not' wait upon 'I would,'
Like the poor cat i' the adage?
MACB. Prithee, peace: 45
I dare do all that may become a man;
Who dares do more is none.
LADY M. What beast was't then

That made you break this enterprise to me?
When you durst do it, then you were a man;
And, to be more than what you were, you
would $_{50}$
Be so much more the man. Nor time nor
place
Did then adhere, and yet you would make
both:
They have made themselves, and that their
fitness now
Does unmake you. I have given suck,
and know
How tender 'tis to love the babe that milks
me: $_{55}$
I would, while it was smiling in my face,
Have pluck'd my nipple from his boneless
gums,
And dash'd the brains out, had I so sworn
as you
Have done to this.
MACB. If we should fail?
LADY M. We fail!
But screw your courage to the
sticking-place, $_{60}$
And we'll not fail. When Duncan is asleep—
Whereto the rather shall his day's hard
journey
Soundly invite him—his two chamberlains
Will I with wine and wassail so convince
That memory, the warder of the brain, $_{65}$
Shall be a fume, and the receipt of reason
A limbec only: when in swinish sleep
Their drenched natures lie as in a death,
What cannot you and I perform upon
The unguarded Duncan? what not put
upon $_{70}$
His spongy officers, who shall bear the guilt

Of our great quell?
MACB. Bring forth men-children only;
For thy undaunted mettle should compose
Nothing but males. Will it not be received,
When we have mark'd with blood those
    sleepy two 75
Of his own chamber, and used their very
    daggers,
That they have done't?
LADY M. Who dares receive it other,
As we shall make our griefs and clamour roar
Upon his death?
MACB. I am settled, and bend up
Each corporal agent to this terrible feat. 80
Away, and mock the time with fairest show:
False face must hide what the false heart doth
    know.

(Exeunt.)

ACT II.

SCENE I. INVERNESS. COURT OF MACBETH'S CASTLE.

(Enter Banquo, and Fleance bearing a torch before him.)

BAN. How goes the night, boy?
FLE. The moon is down; I have not heard the
    clock.
BAN. And she goes down at twelve.
FLE. I take't, 'tis later, sir.
BAN. Hold, take my sword. There's
    husbandry in heaven,
Their candles are all out. Take thee that too. 5
A heavy summons lies like lead upon me,
And yet I would not sleep. Merciful powers,
Restrain in me the cursed thoughts that
    nature
Gives way to in repose!

(Enter Macbeth, and a Servant with a torch.)

Give me my sword.
Who's there? 10

MACB. A friend.

BAN. What, sir, not yet at rest? The king's
    a-bed:
He hath been in unusual pleasure, and
Sent forth great largess to your offices:
This diamond he greets your wife withal, 15
By the name of most kind hostess; and
    shut up
In measureless content.

MACB. Being unprepared,
Our will became the servant to defect,
Which else should free have wrought.

BAN. All's well.
I dreamt last night of the three weird
    sisters: 20
To you they have show'd some truth.

MACB. I think not of them:
Yet, when we can entreat an hour to serve,
We would spend it in some words upon that
    business,
If you would grant the time.

BAN. At your kind'st leisure.

MACB. If you shall cleave to my consent,
    when 'tis 25
It shall make honour for you.

BAN. So I lose none
In seeking to augment it, but still keep
My bosom franchised and allegiance clear,
I shall be counsell'd.

MACB. Good repose the while!

BAN. Thanks, sir: the like to you! 30

(Exeunt Banquo and Fleance.

MACB. Go bid thy mistress, when my drink is
    ready,

She strike upon the bell. Get thee to bed.
   (Exit Servant.)
Is this a dagger which I see before me,
The handle toward my hand? Come, let me
   clutch thee.
I have thee not, and yet I see thee still. 35
Art thou not, fatal vision, sensible
To feeling as to sight? or art thou but
A dagger of the mind, a false creation,
Proceeding from the heat-oppressed brain?
I see thee yet, in form as palpable 40
As this which now I draw.
Thou marshall'st me the way that I was
   going;
And such an instrument I was to use.
Mine eyes are made the fools o' the other
   senses,
Or else worth all the rest: I see thee still; 45
And on thy blade and dudgeon gouts of
   blood,
Which was not so before. There's no such
   thing:
It is the bloody business which informs
Thus to mine eyes. Now o'er the one half-
   world
Nature seems dead, and wicked dreams
   abuse 50
The curtain'd sleep; witchcraft celebrates
Pale Hecate's offerings; and wither'd
   murder,
Alarum'd by his sentinel, the wolf,
Whose howl's his watch, thus with his stealthy
   pace,
With Tarquin's ravishing strides, towards his
   design 55
Moves like a ghost. Thou sure and firm-set
   earth,

Hear not my steps, which way they walk,
    for fear
Thy very stones prate of my whereabout,
And take the present horror from the time,
Which now suits with it. Whiles I threat, he
    lives: 60
Words to the heat of deeds too cold breath
    gives.

                    (A bell rings.)

I go, and it is done: the bell invites me.
Hear it not, Duncan, for it is a knell
That summons thee to heaven, or to hell.
    (Exit.)

SCENE II. THE SAME

(Enter Lady Macbeth.)

    LADY M. That which hath made them drunk
    hath made me bold;
What hath quench'd them hath given me fire.
    Hark! Peace!
It was the owl that shriek'd, the fatal bellman,
Which gives the stern'st good-night. He is
    about it:
The doors are open, and the surfeited
    grooms 5
Do mock their charge with snores: I have
    drugg'd their possets,
That death and nature do contend about
    them,
Whether they live or die.
    MACB. *(Within)* Who's there? what, ho!
    LADY M. Alack, I am afraid they have
    awaked

And 'tis not done: the attempt and not the
    deed 10
Confounds us. Hark! I laid their daggers
    ready;
He could not miss 'em. Had he not
    resembled
My father as he slept, I had done 't.

(Enter Macbeth.)

My husband!
MACB. I have done the deed. Didst thou not
    hear a noise?
LADY M. I heard the owl scream and the
    crickets cry. 15
Did not you speak?
MACB. When?
LADY M. Now.
MACB. As I descended?
LADY M. Ay.
MACB. Hark!
Who lies i' the second chamber?
LADY M. Donalbain.
MACB. This is a sorry sight. *(Looking on his
    hands.)* 20
LADY M. A foolish thought, to say a sorry
    sight.
MACB. There's one did laugh in's sleep, and
    one cried 'Murder!'
That they did wake each other: I stood and
    heard them:
But they did say their prayers, and address'd
    them
Again to sleep.
LADY M. There are two lodged together. 25
MACB. One cried 'God bless us!' and 'Amen'
    the other,

As they had seen me with these hangman's
    hands:
Listening their fear, I could not say 'Amen,'
When they did say 'God bless us!'
LADY M. Consider it not so deeply. 30
MACB. But wherefore could not I pronounce
    'Amen'?
I had most need of blessing, and 'Amen'
Stuck in my throat.
LADY M. These deeds must not be thought
After these ways; so, it will make us mad.
MACB. Methought I heard a voice cry 'Sleep
    no more! 35
Macbeth does murder sleep'—the innocent
    sleep,
Sleep that knits up the ravell'd sleave of
    care,
The death of each day's life, sore labour's
    bath,
Balm of hurt minds, great nature's second
    course,
Chief nourisher in life's feast,—
LADY M. What do you mean? 40
MACB. Still it cried 'Sleep no more!' to all the
    house:
'Glamis hath murder'd sleep, and therefore
    Cawdor
Shall sleep no more: Macbeth shall sleep no
    more.'
LADY M. Who was it that thus cried? Why,
    worthy thane,
You do unbend your noble strength, to
    think 45
So brainsickly of things. Go get some water,
And wash this filthy witness from your hand.
Why did you bring these daggers from the
    place?

They must lie there: go carry them, and
    smear
The sleepy grooms with blood.

MACB. I'll go no more: 50
I am afraid to think what I have done;
Look on 't again I dare not.

LADY M. Infirm of purpose!
Give me the daggers: the sleeping and
    the dead
Are but as pictures: 'tis the eye of childhood
That fears a painted devil. If he do bleed, 55
I'll gild the faces of the grooms withal,
For it must seem their guilt. *(Exit. Knocking
    within.)*

MACB. Whence is that knocking?
How is 't with me, when every noise
    appals me?
What hands are here? ha! they pluck out
    mine eyes!
Will all great Neptune's ocean wash this
    blood 60
Clean from my hand? No; this my hand will
    rather
The multitudinous seas incarnadine,
Making the green one red.

(Re-enter Lady Macbeth.)

LADY M. My hands are of your colour, but I
    shame
To wear a heart so white. *(Knocking within)* I
    hear a knocking 65
At the south entry: retire we to our chamber:
A little water clears us of this deed:
How easy is it then! Your constancy
Hath left you unattended. *(Knocking within)*
    Hark! more knocking:

Get on your nightgown, lest occasion call
us [70]
And show us to be watchers: be not lost
So poorly in your thoughts.
MACB. To know my deed, 'twere best not
know myself.

(Knocking within.)

Wake Duncan with thy knocking! I would
thou couldst!

(Exeunt.)

SCENE III. THE SAME: (ENTER A PORTER. KNOCKING WITHIN.)

PORTER. Here's a knocking indeed! If a man
were porter
of hell-gate, he should have old turning the
key. *(Knocking within)*
Knock, knock, knock! Who's there, i' the
name of
Beelzebub? Here's a farmer, that hanged
himself on th' expectation
of plenty: come in time; have napkins enow
about [5]
you; here you'll sweat for't. *(Knocking within.)*
Knock,
knock! Who's there, in th' other devil's name?
Faith,
here's an equivocator, that could swear in
both the scales
against either scale; who committed treason
enough for

God's sake, yet could not equivocate to
     heaven: O, come $_{10}$
in, equivocator. *(Knocking within.)* Knock,
     knock, knock!
Who's there? Faith, here's an English tailor
     come hither,
for stealing out of a French hose: come in,
     tailor; here you
may roast your goose. *(Knocking within.)*
     Knock, knock;
never at quiet! What are you? But this place is
     too cold $_{15}$
for hell. I'll devil-porter it no further: I had
     thought to
have let in some of all professions, that go the
     primrose
way to the everlasting bonfire. *(Knocking
     within.)* Anon,
anon! I pray you, remember the porter. *(Opens
     the gate.)*

(Enter Macduff and Lennox.)

MACD. Was it so late, friend, ere you went to
     bed, $_{20}$
That you do lie so late?
PORT. Faith, sir, we were carousing till the
     second cock:
and drink, sir, is a great provoker of three
     things.
MACD. What three things does drink
     especially provoke?
PORT. Marry, sir, nose-painting, sleep and
     urine. Lechery, $_{25}$
sir, it provokes and unprovokes; it provokes
     the desire,

but it takes away the performance: therefore
    much drink
may be said to be an equivocator with
    lechery: it makes
him and it mars him; it sets him on and it
    takes him off;
it persuades him and disheartens him; makes
    him stand 30
to and not stand to; in conclusion,
    equivocates him in a
sleep, and giving him the lie, leaves him.
MACD. I believe drink gave thee the lie last
    night.
PORT. That it did, sir, i' the very throat on
    me: but I
requited him for his lie, and, I think, being
    too strong for 35
him, though he took up my legs sometime, yet
    I made a
shift to cast him.
MACD. Is thy master stirring?

(Enter Macbeth.)

Our knocking has awaked him; here he
    comes.
LEN. Good morrow, noble sir.
MACB. Good morrow, both. 40
MACD. Is the king stirring, worthy thane?
MACB. Not yet.
MACD. He did command me to call timely
    on him:
I have almost slipp'd the hour.
MACB. I'll bring you to him.
MACD. I know this is a joyful trouble to you;
But yet 'tis one. 45

MACB. The labour we delight in physics
    pain.
This is the door.
MACD. I'll make so bold to call,
For 'tis my limited service. *(Exit.)*
LEN. Goes the king hence to-day?
MACB. He does: he did appoint so.
LEN. The night has been unruly: where we
    lay, 50
Our chimneys were blown down, and, as
    they say,
Lamentings heard i' the air, strange screams
    of death,
And prophesying with accents terrible
Of dire combustion and confused events
New hatch'd to the woful time: the obscure
    bird 55
Clamour'd the livelong night: some say, the
    earth
Was feverous and did shake.
MACB. Twas a rough night.
LEN. My young remembrance cannot parallel
A fellow to it.

(Re-enter Macduff)

MACD. O horror, horror, horror! Tongue nor
    heart 60
Cannot conceive nor name thee.
MACB. }
LEN. } What's the matter?
MACD. Confusion now hath made his
    masterpiece.
Most sacrilegious murder hath broke ope
The Lord's anointed temple, and stole thence
The life o' the building.

MACB. What is't you say? the life? 65
LEN. Mean you his majesty?
MACD. Approach the chamber, and destroy
    your sight
With a new Gorgon: do not bid me speak;
See, and then speak yourselves. *(Exeunt*
    Macbeth and Lennox.)
Awake, awake!
Ring the alarum-bell. Murder and treason! 70
Banquo and Donalbain! Malcolm! awake!
Shake off this downy sleep, death's
    counterfeit,
And look on death itself! up, up, and see
The great doom's image! Malcolm! Banquo!
As from your graves rise up, and walk like
    sprites, 75
To countenance this horror. Ring the bell.
    (Bell rings.)

(Enter Lady Macbeth.)

LADY M. What's the business,
That such a hideous trumpet calls to parley
The sleepers of the house? speak, speak!
MACD. O gentle lady,
'Tis not for you to hear what I can speak: 80
The repetition, in a woman's ear,
Would murder as it fell.

(Enter Banquo.)

O Banquo, Banquo!
Our royal master's murder'd.
LADY M. Woe, alas!
What, in our house?
BAN. Too cruel any where.
Dear Duff, I prithee, contradict thyself, 85

And say it is not so.

(Re-enter Macbeth and Lennox, with Ross.)

MACB. Had I but died an hour before this
    chance,
I had lived a blessed time; for from this
    instant
There's nothing serious in mortality:
All is but toys: renown and grace is dead; 90
The wine of life is drawn, and the mere lees
Is left this vault to brag of.

(Enter Malcolm and Donalbain.)

DON. What is amiss?
MACB. You are, and do not know't:
The spring, the head, the fountain of your
    blood
Is stopp'd; the very source of it is stopp'd. 95
MACD. Your royal father's murder'd.
MAL. O, by whom?
LEN. Those of his chamber, as it seem'd, had
    done't:
Their hands and faces were all badged with
    blood;
So were their daggers, which unwiped we
    found
Upon their pillows: 100
They stared, and were distracted; no
    man's life
Was to be trusted with them.
MACB. O, yet I do repent me of my fury,
That I did kill them.
MACD. Wherefore did you so?
MACB. Who can be wise, amazed, temperate
    and furious, 105

Loyal and neutral, in a moment? No man:
The expedition of my violent love
Outrun the pauser reason. Here lay Duncan,
His silver skin laced with his golden blood,
And his gash'd stabs look'd like a breach in
    nature 110
For ruin's wasteful entrance: there, the
    murderers,
Steep'd in the colours of their trade, their
    daggers
Unmannerly breech'd with gore: who could
    refrain,
That had a heart to love, and in that heart
Courage to make's love known?
LADY M. Help me hence, ho! 115
MACD. Look to the lady.
MAL. *(Aside to Don.)* Why do we hold our
    tongues,
That most may claim this argument for ours?
DON. *(Aside to Mal.)* What should be spoken
    here, where our fate,
Hid in an auger-hole, may rush, and seize us?
Let's away; 120
Our tears are not yet brew'd.
MAL. *(Aside to Don.)* Nor our strong sorrow
Upon the foot of motion.
BAN. Look to the lady:

          (Lady Macbeth is carried out.)

And when we have our naked frailties hid,
That suffer in exposure, let us meet,
And question this most bloody piece of
    work, 125
To know it further. Fears and scruples
    shake us:
In the great hand of God I stand, and thence

Against the undivulged pretence I fight
Of treasonous malice.
MACD. And so do I.
ALL. So *ALL*.
MACB. Let's briefly put on manly
    readiness,₁₃₀
And meet i' the hall together.
ALL. Well contented.

(Exeunt all but Malcolm and Donalbain.)

MAL. What will you do? Let's not consort
    with them:
To show an unfelt sorrow is an office
Which the false man does easy. I'll to
    England.
DON. To Ireland, I; our separated fortune ₁₃₅
Shall keep us both the safer: where we are
There's daggers in men's smiles: the near in
    blood,
The nearer bloody.
MAL. This murderous shaft that's shot
Hath not yet lighted, and our safest way
Is to avoid the aim. Therefore to horse; ₁₄₀
And let us not be dainty of leave-taking,
But shift away: there's warrant in that theft
Which steals itself when there's no mercy left.

(Exeunt.)

SCENE IV. OUTSIDE MACBETH'S CASTLE

(Enter Ross with an old Man.)

  OLD M. Threescore and ten I can remember
    well:
Within the volume of which time I have seen

Hours dreadful and things strange, but this
    sore night
Hath trifled former knowings.
Ross. Ah, good father,
Thou seest, the heavens, as troubled with
    man's act, 5
Threaten his bloody stage: by the clock
    'tis day,
And yet dark night strangles the travelling
    lamp:
Is't night's predominance, or the day's shame,
That darkness does the face of earth entomb,
When living light should kiss it?
Old M. 'Tis unnatural, 10
Even like the deed that's done. On Tuesday
    last
A falcon towering in her pride of place
Was by a mousing owl hawk'd at and kill'd.
Ross. And Duncan's horses—a thing most
    strange and certain—
Beauteous and swift, the minions of their
    race, 15
Turn'd wild in nature, broke their stalls,
    flung out,
Contending 'gainst obedience, as they
    would make
War with mankind.
Old M. 'Tis said they eat each other.
Ross. They did so, to the amazement of
    mine eyes,
That look'd upon't.

(Enter Macduff.)

Here comes the good Macduff. 20
How goes the world, sir, now?
Macd. Why, see you not?

40

Ross. Is't known who did this more than
    bloody deed?

Macd. Those that Macbeth hath slain.

Ross. Alas, the day!

What good could they pretend?

Macd. They were suborn'd:

Malcolm and Donalbain, the king's two
    sons, 25

Are stol'n away and fled, which puts
    upon them

Suspicion of the deed.

Ross. 'Gainst nature still:

Thriftless ambition, that wilt ravin up

Thine own life's means! Then 'tis most like

The sovereignty will fall upon Macbeth. 30

Macd. He is already named, and gone to
    Scone

To be invested.

Ross. Where is Duncan's body?

Macd. Carried to Colme-kill,

The sacred storehouse of his predecessors

And guardian of their bones.

Ross. Will you to Scone? 35

Macd. No, cousin, I'll to Fife.

Ross. Well, I will thither.

Macd. Well, may you see things well done
    there: adieu!

Lest our old robes sit easier than our new!

Ross. Farewell, father.

Old M. God's benison go with you, and
    with those 40

That would make good of bad and friends of
    foes!

(Exeunt.)

ACT III.

SCENE I. FORRES. THE PALACE.

(Enter Banquo.)

BAN. Thou hast it now: king, Cawdor,
    Glamis, all,
As the weird women promised, and I fear
Thou play'dst most foully for't: yet it was said
It should not stand in thy posterity,
But that myself should be the root and
    father 5
Of many kings. If there come truth from
    them—
As upon thee, Macbeth, their speeches
    shine—
Why, by the verities on thee made good,
May they not be my oracles as well
And set me up in hope? But hush, no more. 10

(Sennet sounded. Enter Macbeth, as king; Lady Macbeth, as queen; Lennox, Ross, Lords, Ladies, and Attendants.)

MACB. Here's our chief guest.

43

LADY M. If he had been forgotten,
It had been as a gap in our great feast,
And all-thing unbecoming.
MACB. To-night we hold a solemn supper, sir,
And I'll request your presence.
BAN. Let your highness $_{15}$
Command upon me, to the which my duties
Are with a most indissoluble tie
For ever knit.
MACB. Ride you this afternoon?
BAN. Ay, my good lord.
MACB. We should have else desired your
    good advice, $_{20}$
Which still hath been both grave and
    prosperous,
In this day's council; but we'll take to-
    morrow.
Is't far you ride?
BAN. As far, my lord, as will fill up the time
'Twixt this and supper: go not my horse the
    better, $_{25}$
I must become a borrower of the night
For a dark hour or twain.
MACB. Fail not our feast.
BAN. My lord, I will not.
MACB. We hear our bloody cousins are
    bestow'd
In England and in Ireland, not confessing $_{30}$
Their cruel parricide, filling their hearers
With strange invention: but of that to-
    morrow,
When therewithal we shall have cause of state
Craving us jointly. Hie you to horse: adieu,
Till you return at night. Goes Fleance with
    you? $_{35}$
BAN. Ay, my good lord: our time does call
    upon 's.

MACB. I wish your horses swift and sure of
    foot,
And so I do commend you to their backs.
Farewell. *(Exit Banquo.)*
Let every man be master of his time 40
Till seven at night; to make society
The sweeter welcome, we will keep ourself
Till supper-time alone: while then, God be
    with you!

       (Exeunt all but Macbeth and an Attendant.)

Sirrah, a word with you: attend those men
Our pleasure? 45
ATTEND. They are, my lord, without the
    palace-gate.
MACB. Bring them before us. *(Exit Attendant.)*
To be thus is nothing;
But to be safely thus: our fears in Banquo
Stick deep; and in his royalty of nature
Reigns that which would be fear'd: 'tis much
    he dares, 50
And, to that dauntless temper of his mind,
He hath a wisdom that doth guide his valour
To act in safety. There is none but he
Whose being I do fear: and under him
My Genius is rebuked, as it is said 55
Mark Antony's was by Cæsar. He chid the
    sisters,
When first they put the name of king
    upon me,
And bade them speak to him; then prophet-
    like
They hail'd him father to a line of kings:
Upon my head they placed a fruitless
    crown 60
And put a barren sceptre in my gripe,

Thence to be wrench'd with an unlineal
    hand,
No son of mine succeeding. If 't be so,
For Banquo's issue have I filed my mind;
For them the gracious Duncan have I
    murder'd; 65
Put rancours in the vessel of my peace
Only for them, and mine eternal jewel
Given to the common enemy of man,
To make them kings, the seed of Banquo
    kings!
Rather than so, come, fate, into the list, 70
And champion me to the utterance! Who's
    there?

(Re-enter Attendant, with two Murderers.)

Now go to the door, and stay there till we call.

(Exit Attendant.)

Was it not yesterday we spoke together?
FIRST MUR. It was, so please your highness.
MACB. Well then, now
Have you consider'd of my speeches?
    Know 75
That it was he in the times past which
    held you
So under fortune, which you thought
    had been
Our innocent self: this I made good to you
In our last conference, pass'd in probation
    with you,
How you were borne in hand, how cross'd,
    the instruments, 80
Who wrought with them, and all things else
    that might

To half a soul and to a notion crazed
Say 'Thus did Banquo.'
First Mur. You made it known to us.
Macb. I did so; and went further, which
    is now
Our point of second meeting. Do you find ₈₅
Your patience so predominant in your nature,
That you can let this go? Are you so gospell'd,
To pray for this good man and for his issue,
Whose heavy hand hath bow'd you to the
    grave
And beggar'd yours for ever?
First Mur. We are men, my liege. ₉₀
Macb. Ay, in the catalogue ye go for men;
As hounds and greyhounds, mongrels,
    spaniels, curs,
Shoughs, water-rugs and demi-wolves, are
    clept
All by the name of dogs: the valued file
Distinguishes the swift, the slow, the subtle, ₉₅
The housekeeper, the hunter, every one
According to the gift which bounteous nature
Hath in him closed; whereby he does receive
Particular addition, from the bill
That writes them all alike: and so of men. ₁₀₀
Now if you have a station in the file,
Not i' the worst rank of manhood, say it,
And I will put that business in your bosoms
Whose execution takes your enemy off,
Grapples you to the heart and love of us, ₁₀₅
Who wear our health but sickly in his life,
Which in his death were perfect.
Sec. Mur. I am one, my liege,
Whom the vile blows and buffets of the world
Have so incensed that I am reckless what
I do to spite the world.
First Mur. And I another ₁₁₀

So weary with disasters, tugg'd with fortune,
That I would set my life on any chance,
To mend it or be rid on 't.
MACB. Both of you
Know Banquo was your enemy.
BOTH MUR. True, my lord.
MACB. So is he mine, and in such bloody
    distance 115
That every minute of his being thrusts
Against my near'st of life: and though I could
With barefaced power sweep him from my
    sight
And bid my will avouch it, yet I must not,
For certain friends that are both his and
    mine, 120
Whose loves I may not drop, but wail his fall
Who I myself struck down: and thence it is
That I to your assistance do make love,
Masking the business from the common eye
For sundry weighty reasons.
SEC. MUR. We shall, my lord, 125
Perform what you command us.
FIRST MUR. Though our lives—
MACB. Your spirits shine through you.
    Within this hour at most
I will advise you where to plant yourselves,
Acquaint you with the perfect spy o' the time,
The moment on 't; for 't must be done
    to-night, 130
And something from the palace; always
    thought
That I require a clearness: and with him—
To leave no rubs nor botches in the work—
Fleance his son, that keeps him company,
Whose absence is no less material to me 135
Than is his father's, must embrace the fate
Of that dark hour. Resolve yourselves apart:

I'll come to you anon.
BOTH MUR. We are resolved, my lord.
MACB. I'll call upon you straight: abide
    within.

(Exeunt Murderers.)

It is concluded: Banquo, thy soul's flight, $_{140}$
If it find heaven, must find it out to-night.

(Exit.)

SCENE II. THE PALACE

(Enter Lady Macbeth and a Servant.)

LADY M. Is Banquo gone from court?
SERV. Ay, madam, but returns again to-night.
LADY M. Say to the king, I would attend his
    leisure
For a few words.
SERV. Madam, I will. *(Exit.)*
LADY M. Nought's had, all's spent,
Where our desire is got without content: $_5$
'Tis safer to be that which we destroy
Than by destruction dwell in doubtful joy.

(Enter Macbeth.)

How now, my lord! why do you keep alone,
Of sorriest fancies your companions making;
Using those thoughts which should indeed
    have died $_{10}$
With them they think on? Things without all
    remedy
Should be without regard: what's done is
    done.

MACB. We have scotch'd the snake, not
 kill'd it:
She'll close and be herself, whilst our poor
 malice
Remains in danger of her former tooth. 15
But let the frame of things disjoint, both the
 worlds suffer,
Ere we will eat our meal in fear, and sleep
In the affliction of these terrible dreams
That shake us nightly: better be with the
 dead,
Whom we, to gain our peace, have sent to
 peace, 20
Than on the torture of the mind to lie
In restless ecstasy. Duncan is in his grave;
After life's fitful fever he sleeps well;
Treason has done his worst: nor steel, nor
 poison,
Malice domestic, foreign levy, nothing, 25
Can touch him further.
LADY M. Come on;
Gentle my lord, sleek o'er your rugged looks;
Be bright and jovial among your guests to-
 night.
MACB. So shall I, love; and so, I pray, be you:
Let your remembrance apply to Banquo; 30
Present him eminence, both with eye and
 tongue:
Unsafe the while, that we
Must lave our honours in these flattering
 streams,
And make our faces visards to our hearts,
Disguising what they are.
LADY M. You must leave this. 35
MACB. O, full of scorpions is my mind, dear
 wife!

Thou know'st that Banquo, and his Fleance, lives.

LADY M. But in them nature's copy's not eterne.

MACB. There's comfort yet; they are assailable;

Then be thou jocund: ere the bat hath flown 40

His cloister'd flight; ere to black Hecate's summons

The shard-borne beetle with his drowsy hums

Hath rung night's yawning peal, there shall be done

A deed of dreadful note.

LADY M. What's to be done?

MACB. Be innocent of the knowledge, dearest chuck, 45

Till thou applaud the deed. Come, seeling night,

Scarf up the tender eye of pitiful day,

And with thy bloody and invisible hand

Cancel and tear to pieces that great bond

Which keeps me pale! Light thickens, and the crow 50

Makes wing to the rooky wood:

Good things of day begin to droop and drowse,

Whiles night's black agents to their preys do rouse.

Thou marvell'st at my words: but hold thee still;

Things bad begun make strong themselves by ill: 55

So, prithee, go with me. *(Exeunt.)*

SCENE III. A PARK NEAR THE PALACE:
(ENTER THREE MURDERERS.)

FIRST MUR. But who did bid thee join
    with us?
THIRD MUR. Macbeth.
SEC. MUR. He needs not our mistrust; since
    he delivers
Our offices, and what we have to do,
To the direction just.
FIRST MUR. Then stand with us.
The west yet glimmers with some streaks of
    day: 5
Now spurs the lated traveller apace
To gain the timely inn, and near approaches
The subject of our watch.
THIRD MUR. Hark! I hear horses.
BAN. *(Within)* Give us a light there, ho!
SEC. MUR. Then 'tis he: the rest
That are within the note of expectation 10
Already are i' the court.
FIRST MUR. His horses go about.
THIRD MUR. Almost a mile: but he does
    usually—
So all men do—from hence to the palace gate
Make it their walk.
SEC. MUR. A light, a light!

(Enter Banquo, and Fleance with a torch.)

THIRD MUR. 'Tis he.
FIRST MUR. Stand to 't. 15
BAN. It will be rain to-night.
FIRST MUR. Let it come down.

(They set upon Banquo.)

BAN. O, treachery! Fly, good Fleance, fly,
fly, fly!
Thou mayst revenge. O slave! *(Dies. Fleance
escapes.)*
THIRD MUR. Who did strike out the light?
FIRST MUR. Was't not the way?
THIRD MUR. There's but one down; the son
is fled.
SEC. MUR. We have lost
Best half of our affair.
FIRST MUR. Well, let's away and say how
much is done. *(Exeunt.)*

SCENE IV. HALL IN THE PALACE

*(A banquet prepared. Enter Macbeth, Lady Macbeth, Ross,
Lennox, Lords, and Attendants.)*

MACB. You know your own degrees; sit
down: at first
And last the hearty welcome.
LORDS. Thanks to your majesty.
MACB. Ourself will mingle with society
And play the humble host.
Our hostess keeps her state, but in best time
We will require her welcome.
LADY M. Pronounce it for me, sir, to all our
friends,
For my heart speaks they are welcome.

(Enter first Murderer to the door.)

MACB. See, they encounter thee with their
hearts' thanks.
Both sides are even: here I'll sit i' the midst:
Be large in mirth; anon we'll drink a measure

The table round. *(Approaching the door)* There's
blood upon thy face.

MUR. 'Tis Banquo's then.

MACB. 'Tis better thee without than he
within.

Is he dispatch'd? 15

MUR. My lord, his throat is cut; that I did
for him.

MACB. Thou art the best o' the cut-throats:
yet he's good

That did the like for Fleance: if thou didst it,

Thou art the nonpareil.

MUR. Most royal sir,

Fleance is 'scaped. 20

MACB. *(Aside)* Then comes my fit again: I
had else been perfect,

Whole as the marble, founded as the rock,

As broad and general as the casing air:

But now I am cabin'd, cribb'd, confined,
bound in

To saucy doubts and fears.—But Banquo's
safe? 25

MUR. Ay, my good lord: safe in a ditch he
bides,

With twenty trenched gashes on his head;

The least a death to nature.

MACB. Thanks for that.

(Aside) There the grown serpent lies; the
worm that's fled

Hath nature that in time will venom breed, 30

No teeth for the present. Get thee gone: to-
morrow

We'll hear ourselves again. *(Exit Murderer.)*

LADY M. My royal lord,

You do not give the cheer: the feast is sold

That is not often vouch'd, while 'tis a-
making,

'Tis given with welcome: to feed were best at
    home; 35
From thence the sauce to meat is ceremony;
Meeting were bare without it.
MACB. Sweet remembrancer!
Now good digestion wait on appetite,
And health on both!
LEN. May't please your highness sit.

(The Ghost of Banquo enters, and sits in Macbeth's place.)

MACB. Here had we now our country's
    honour roof'd, 40
Were the graced person of our Banquo
    present;
Who may I rather challenge for unkindness
Than pity for mischance!
ROSS. His absence, sir,
Lays blame upon his promise. Please't your
    highness
To grace us with your royal company. 45
MACB. The table's full.
LEN. Here is a place reserved, sir.
MACB. Where?
LEN. Here, my good lord. What is't that
    moves your highness?
MACB. Which of you have done this?
Lords. What, my good lord?
MACB. Thou canst not say I did it: never
    shake 50
Thy gory locks at me.
ROSS. Gentlemen, rise; his highness is not
    well.
LADY M. Sit, worthy friends: my lord is often
    thus,
And hath been from his youth: pray you, keep
    seat;

The fit is momentary; upon a thought $_{55}$
He will again be well: if much you note him,
You shall offend him and extend his passion:
Feed, and regard him not. Are you a man?

MACB. Ay, and a bold one, that dare look
on that
Which might appal the devil.

LADY M. O proper stuff! $_{60}$
This is the very painting of your fear:
This is the air-drawn dagger which, you said,
Led you to Duncan. O, these flaws and starts,
Impostors to true fear, would well become
A woman's story at a winter's fire, $_{65}$
Authorized by her grandam. Shame itself!
Why do you make such faces? When all's
done,
You look but on a stool.

MACB. Prithee, see there! behold! look! lo!
how say you?
Why, what care I? If thou canst nod, speak
too. $_{70}$
If charnel-houses and our graves must send
Those that we bury back, our monuments
Shall be the maws of kites. *(Exit Ghost.)*

LADY M. What, quite unmann'd in folly?

MACB. If I stand here, I saw him.

LADY M. Fie, for shame!

MACB. Blood hath been shed ere now, i' the
olden time,$_{75}$
Ere humane statute purged the gentle weal;
Ay, and since too, murders have been
perform'd
Too terrible for the ear: the time has been,
That, when the brains were out, the man
would die,
And there an end; but now they rise again, $_{80}$

With twenty mortal murders on their crowns,
And push us from our stools: this is more
    strange
Than such a murder is.
LADY M. My worthy lord,
Your noble friends do lack you.
MACB. I do forget.
Do not muse at me, my most worthy
    friends; 85
I have a strange infirmity, which is nothing
To those that know me. Come, love and
    health to all;
Then I'll sit down. Give me some wine, fill
    full.
I drink to the general joy o' the whole table,
And to our dear friend Banquo, whom we
    miss; 90
Would he were here! to all and him we thirst,
And all to all.
LORDS. Our duties, and the pledge.

(Re-enter Ghost.)

MACB. Avaunt! and quit my sight! let the
    earth hide thee!
Thy bones are marrowless, thy blood is cold;
Thou hast no speculation in those eyes 95
Which thou dost glare with.
LADY M. Think of this, good peers,
But as a thing of custom: 'tis no other;
Only it spoils the pleasure of the time.
MACB. What man dare, I dare:
Approach thou like the rugged Russian
    bear, 100
The arm'd rhinoceros, or the Hyrcan tiger;
Take any shape but that, and my firm nerves

Shall never tremble: or be alive again,
And dare me to the desert with thy sword;
If trembling I inhabit then, protest me 105
The baby of a girl. Hence, horrible shadow!
Unreal mockery, hence! *(Exit Ghost.)*
Why, so: being gone,
I am a man again. Pray you, sit still.
LADY M. You have displaced the mirth,
 broke the good meeting,
With most admired disorder.
MACB. Can such things be, 110
And overcome us like a summer's cloud,
Without our special wonder? You make me
 strange
Even to the disposition that I owe,
When now I think you can behold such
 sights,
And keep the natural ruby of your cheeks, 115
When mine is blanch'd with fear.
ROSS. What sights, my lord?
LADY M. I pray you, speak not; he grows
 worse and worse;
Question enrages him: at once, good night:
Stand not upon the order of your going,
But go at once.
LEN. Good night; and better health 120
Attend his majesty!
LADY M. A kind good night to all!

(Exeunt all but Macbeth and Lady M.)

MACB. It will have blood: they say blood will
 have blood:
Stones have been known to move and trees to
 speak;
Augures and understood relations have

By maggot-pies and choughs and rooks
　　brought forth 125
The secret'st man of blood. What is the
　　night?

LADY M. Almost at odds with morning,
　　which is which.

MACB. How say'st thou, that Macduff denies
　　his person
At our great bidding?

LADY M. Did you send to him, sir?

MACB. I hear it by the way, but I will send: 130
There's not a one of them but in his house
I keep a servant fee'd. I will to-morrow,
And betimes I will, to the weird sisters:
More shall they speak, for now I am bent to
　　know,
By the worst means, the worst. For mine own
　　good 135
All causes shall give way: I am in blood
Stepp'd in so far that, should I wade no more,
Returning were as tedious as go o'er:
Strange things I have in head that will to
　　hand,
Which must be acted ere they may be
　　scann'd. 140

LADY M. You lack the season of all natures,
　　sleep.

MACB. Come, we'll to sleep. My strange and
　　self-abuse
Is the initiate fear that wants hard use:
We are yet but young in deed. *(Exeunt.)*

SCENE V. A HEATH: (THUNDER. ENTER THE THREE WITCHES, MEETING HECATE.)

FIRST WITCH. Why, how now, Hecate! you
    look angerly.
HEC. Have I not reason, beldams as you are,
Saucy and over-bold? How did you dare
To trade and traffic with Macbeth
In riddles and affairs of death; 5
And I, the mistress of your charms,
The close contriver of all harms,
Was never call'd to bear my part,
Or show the glory of our art?
And, which is worse, all you have done 10
Hath been but for a wayward son,
Spiteful and wrathful; who, as others do,
Loves for his own ends, not for you.
But make amends now: get you gone,
And at the pit of Acheron 15
Meet me i' the morning: thither he
Will come to know his destiny:
Your vessels and your spells provide,
Your charms and every thing beside.
I am for the air; this night I'll spend 20
Unto a dismal and a fatal end:
Great business must be wrought ere noon:
Upon the corner of the moon
There hangs a vaporous drop profound;
I'll catch it ere it come to ground: 25
And that distill'd by magic sleights
Shall raise such artificial sprites
As by the strength of their illusion
Shall draw him on to his confusion:
He shall spurn fate, scorn death, and bear 30
His hopes 'bove wisdom, grace and fear:
And you all know security

Is mortals' chiefest enemy.
*(Music and a song within: 'Come away, come
    away,' &c.)*
Hark! I am call'd; my little spirit, see,
Sits in a foggy cloud, and stays for me.
    (Exit.) 35
FIRST WITCH. Come, let's make haste; she'll
    soon be back again. *(Exeunt.)*

SCENE VI. FORRES. THE PALACE

(Enter Lennox and another Lord.)

LEN. My former speeches have but hit your
    thoughts,
Which can interpret farther: only I say
Things have been strangely borne. The
    gracious Duncan
Was pitied of Macbeth: marry, he was dead:
And the right-valiant Banquo walk'd too
    late; 5
Whom, you may say, if't please you, Fleance
    kill'd,
For Fleance fled: men must not walk too
    late.
Who cannot want the thought, how
    monstrous
It was for Malcolm and for Donalbain
To kill their gracious father? damned fact! 10
How it did grieve Macbeth! did he not
    straight,
In pious rage, the two delinquents tear,
That were the slaves of drink and thralls of
    sleep?
Was not that nobly done? Ay, and wisely too;
For 'twould have anger'd any heart alive 15
To hear the men deny 't. So that, I say,

He has borne all things well: and I do think
That, had he Duncan's sons under his key—
As, an't please heaven, he shall not—they
    should find
What 'twere to kill a father; so should
    Fleance. 20
But, peace! for from broad words, and 'cause
    he fail'd
His presence at the tyrant's feast, I hear,
Macduff lives in disgrace: sir, can you tell
Where he bestows himself?
LORD. The son of Duncan,
From whom this tyrant holds the due of
    birth, 25
Lives in the English court, and is received
Of the most pious Edward with such grace
That the malevolence of fortune nothing
Takes from his high respect. Thither Macduff
Is gone to pray the holy king, upon his aid 30
To wake Northumberland and warlike
    Siward:
That by the help of these, with Him above
To ratify the work, we may again
Give to our tables meat, sleep to our nights,
Free from our feasts and banquets bloody
    knives, 35
Do faithful homage and receive free honours:
All which we pine for now: and this report
Hath so exasperate the king that he
Prepares for some attempt of war.
LEN. Sent he to Macduff?
LORD. He did: and with an absolute 'Sir, not
    I,' 40
The cloudy messenger turns me his back,
And hums, as who should say 'You'll rue
    the time
That clogs me with this answer.'

LEN. And that well might
Advise him to a caution, to hold what
    distance
His wisdom can provide. Some holy angel 45
Fly to the court of England and unfold
His message ere he come, that a swift blessing
May soon return to this our suffering country
Under a hand accursed!
LORD. I'll send my prayers with him.

(Exeunt.)

ACT IV.

SCENE I. A CAVERN. IN THE MIDDLE, A BOILING CAULDRON.

(Thunder. Enter the three Witches.)

> **FIRST WITCH.** Thrice the brinded cat hath
> mew'd.
> **SEC. WITCH.** Thrice and once the hedge-pig
> whined.
> **THIRD WITCH.** Harpier cries ''Tis time, 'tis
> time.'
> **FIRST WITCH.** Round about the cauldron go:
> In the poison'd entrails throw. 5
> Toad, that under cold stone
> Days and nights has thirty one
> Swelter'd venom sleeping got,
> Boil thou first i' the charmed pot.
> **ALL.** Double, double toil and trouble; 10
> Fire burn and cauldron bubble.
> **SEC. WITCH.** Fillet of a fenny snake,
> In the cauldron boil and bake;
> Eye of newt and toe of frog,
> Wool of bat and tongue of dog, 15

Adder's fork and blind-worm's sting,
Lizard's leg and howlet's wing,
For a charm of powerful trouble,
Like a hell-broth boil and bubble.
ALL. Double, double toil and trouble; 20
Fire burn and cauldron bubble.
THIRD WITCH. Scale of dragon, tooth of
    wolf,
Witches' mummy, maw and gulf
Of the ravin'd salt-sea shark,
Root of hemlock digg'd i' the dark, 25
Liver of blaspheming Jew,
Gall of goat and slips of yew
Sliver'd in the moon's eclipse,
Nose of Turk and Tartar's lips,
Finger of birth-strangled babe 30
Ditch-deliver'd by a drab,
Make the gruel thick and slab:
Add thereto a tiger's chaudron,
For the ingredients of our cauldron.
ALL. Double, double toil and trouble; 35
Fire burn and cauldron bubble.
SEC. WITCH. Cool it with a baboon's blood,
Then the charm is firm and good.
(Enter Hecate to the other three Witches.)
HEC. O, well done! I commend your pains;
And every one shall share i' the gains: 40
And now about the cauldron sing,
Like elves and fairies in a ring,
Enchanting all that you put in.

(Music and a song: 'Black spirits,' &c.)

(Hecate retires.)

SEC. WITCH. By the pricking of my thumbs,
Something wicked this way comes: 45

Open, locks,
Whoever knocks!

(Enter Macbeth.)

MACB. How now, you secret, black, and
    midnight hags!
What is't you do?
ALL. A deed without a name.
MACB. I conjure you, by that which you
    profess, 50
Howe'er you come to know it, answer me:
Though you untie the winds, and let them
    fight
Against the churches; though the yesty waves
Confound and swallow navigation up;
Though bladed corn be lodged and trees
    blown down; 55
Though castles topple on their warders'
    heads;
Though palaces and pyramids do slope
Their heads to their foundations; though the
    treasure
Of nature's germins tumble all together,
Even till destruction sicken; answer me 60
To what I ask you.
FIRST WITCH. Speak.
SEC. WITCH. Demand.
THIRD WITCH. We'll answer.
FIRST WITCH. Say, if thou'dst rather hear it
    from our mouths,
Or from our masters?
MACB. Call 'em, let me see 'em.
FIRST WITCH. Pour in sow's blood, that hath
    eaten
Her nine farrow; grease that's sweaten 65
From the murderer's gibbet throw

Into the flame.
ALL. Come, high or low;
Thyself and office deftly show!

(Thunder. First Apparition: an armed Head.)

MACB. Tell me, thou unknown power,—
FIRST WITCH. He knows thy thought:
Hear his speech, but say thou nought. 70
FIRST APP. Macbeth! Macbeth! Macbeth!
    beware Macduff;
Beware the thane of Fife. Dismiss me:
    enough.

(Descends.)

MACB. Whate'er thou art, for thy good
    caution thanks;
Thou hast harp'd my fear aright: but one
    word more,—
FIRST WITCH. He will not be commanded:
    here's another, 75
More potent than the first.

(Thunder. Second Apparition: a bloody Child.)

SEC. APP. Macbeth! Macbeth! Macbeth!
MACB. Had I three ears, I'ld hear thee.
SEC. APP. Be bloody, bold and resolute;
    laugh to scorn
The power of man, for none of woman
    born 80
Shall harm Macbeth. *(Descends.)*
MACB. Then live, Macduff: what need I fear
    of thee?
But yet I'll make assurance double sure,
And take a bond of fate: thou shalt not live;

That I may tell pale-hearted fear it lies, 85
And sleep in spite of thunder.

(Thunder. Third Apparition: a Child crowned, with a tree in his hand.)

What is this,
That rises like the issue of a king,
And wears upon his baby-brow the round
And top of sovereignty?
ALL. Listen, but speak not to 't.
THIRD APP. Be lion-mettled, proud, and take
no care 90
Who chafes, who frets, or where conspirers
are:
Macbeth shall never vanquished be until
Great Birnam wood to high Dunsinane hill
Shall come against him. *(Descends.)*
MACB. That will never be:
Who can impress the forest, bid the tree 95
Unfix his earth-bound root? Sweet
bodements! good!
Rebellion's head, rise never, till the wood
Of Birnam rise, and our high-placed
Macbeth
Shall live the lease of nature, pay his breath
To time and mortal custom. Yet my heart 100
Throbs to know one thing: tell me, if your art
Can tell so much: shall Banquo's issue ever
Reign in this kingdom?
ALL. Seek to know no more.
MACB. I will be satisfied: deny me this,
And an eternal curse fall on you! Let me
know: 105
Why sinks that cauldron? and what noise is
this?

(Hautboys.)

FIRST WITCH. Show*!*
SEC. WITCH. Show!
THIRD WITCH. Show!
ALL. Show his eyes, and grieve his heart; 110
Come like shadows, so depart!

*(A show of eight Kings, the last with a glass in his hand;
Banquo's Ghost following.)*

MACB. Thou art too like the spirit of
    Banquo: down!
Thy crown does sear mine eye-balls. And thy
    hair,
Thou other gold-bound brow, is like the first.
A third is like the former. Filthy hags! 115
Why do you show me this? A fourth! Start,
    eyes!
What, will the line stretch out to the crack of
    doom?
Another yet! A seventh! I'll see no more:
And yet the eighth appears, who bears a glass
Which shows me many more; and some I
    see 120
That two-fold balls and treble sceptres carry:
Horrible sight! Now I see 'tis true;
For the blood-bolter'd Banquo smiles
    upon me,
And points at them for his. What, is this so?

FIRST WITCH. Ay, sir, all this is so: but
    why 125
Stands Macbeth thus amazedly?
Come, sisters, cheer we up his sprites,
And show the best of our delights:
I'll charm the air to give a sound,

70

While you perform your antic round, ₁₃₀
That this great king may kindly say
Our duties did his welcome pay.

(Music. The Witches dance, and then vanish, with Hecate.)

MACB. Where are they? Gone? Let this
    pernicious hour
Stand aye accursed in the calendar!
Come in, without there!

(Enter Lennox.)

LEN. What's your grace's will? ₁₃₅
MACB. Saw you the weird sisters?
LEN. No, my lord.
MACB. Came they not by you?
LEN. No indeed, my lord.
MACB. Infected be the air whereon they ride,
And damn'd all those that trust them! I
    did hear
The galloping of horse: who was't came
    by? ₁₄₀
LEN. 'Tis two or three, my lord, that bring
    you word
Macduff is fled to England.
MACB. Fled to England!
LEN. Ay, my good lord.
MACB. *(Aside)* Time, thou anticipatest my
    dread exploits:
The flighty purpose never is o'ertook ₁₄₅
Unless the deed go with it: from this moment
The very firstlings of my heart shall be
The firstlings of my hand. And even now,
To crown my thoughts with acts, be it thought
    and done:
The castle of Macduff I will surprise; ₁₅₀

Seize upon Fife; give to the edge o' the
    sword
His wife, his babes, and all unfortunate souls
That trace him in his line. No boasting like a
    fool;
This deed I'll do before this purpose cool:
But no more sights!—Where are these
    gentlemen? 155
Come, bring me where they are. *(Exeunt.)*

SCENE II. FIFE. MACDUFF'S CASTLE

(Enter Lady Macduff, her Son, and Ross.)

L. MACD. What had he done, to make him
    fly the land?
Ross. You must have patience, madam.
L. MACD. He had none:
His flight was madness: when our actions
    do not,
Our fears do make us traitors.
Ross. You know not
Whether it was his wisdom or his fear. 5
L. MACD. Wisdom! to leave his wife, to leave
    his babes,
His mansion and his titles, in a place
From whence himself does fly? He loves
    us not;
He wants the natural touch: for the poor
    wren,
The most diminutive of birds, will fight, 10
Her young ones in her nest, against the owl.
All is the fear and nothing is the love;
As little is the wisdom, where the flight
So runs against all reason.
Ross. My dearest coz,
I pray you, school yourself: but, for your

husband, 15
He is noble, wise, judicious, and best knows
The fits o' the season. I dare not speak much
    further:
But cruel are the times, when we are traitors
And do not know ourselves; when we hold
    rumour
From what we fear, yet know not what we
    fear, 20
But float upon a wild and violent sea
Each way and move. I take my leave of you:
Shall not be long but I'll be here again:
Things at the worst will cease, or else climb
    upward
To what they were before. My pretty
    cousin, 25
Blessing upon you!

L. MACD. Father'd he is, and yet he's
    fatherless.

ROSS. I am so much a fool, should I stay
    longer,
It would be my disgrace and your discomfort:
I take my leave at once. *(Exit.)*

L. MACD. Sirrah, your father's dead: 30
And what will you do now? How will you
    live?

SON. As birds do, mother.

L. MACD. What, with worms and flies?

SON. With what I get, I mean; and so do
    they.

L. MACD. Poor bird! thou'ldst never fear the
    net nor lime,
The pitfall nor the gin. 35

SON. Why should I, mother? Poor birds they
    are not set for.
My father is not dead, for all your saying.

L. MACD. Yes, he is dead: how wilt thou do

for a father?

Son. Nay, how will you do for a husband?

L. Macd. Why, I can buy me twenty at any market. 40

Son. Then you'll buy 'em to sell again.

L. Macd. Thou speak'st with all thy wit, and yet, i' faith,

With wit enough for thee.

Son. Was my father a traitor, mother?

L. Macd. Ay, that he was. 45

Son. What is a traitor?

L. Macd. Why, one that swears and lies.

Son. And be all traitors that do so?

L. Macd. Every one that does so is a traitor, and must

be hang'd. 50

Son. And must they all be hang'd that swear and lie?

L. Macd. Every one.

Son. Who must hang them?

L. Macd. Why, the honest men.

Son. Then the liars and swearers are fools; for there 55

are liars and swearers enow to beat the honest men and

hang up them.

L. Macd. Now, God help thee, poor monkey! But how

wilt thou do for a father?

Son. If he were dead, you'd weep for him: if you would 60

not, it were a good sign that I should quickly have a new

father.

L. Macd. Poor prattler, how thou talk'st!

(Enter a Messenger.)

MESS. Bless you, fair dame! I am not to you
    known,
Though in your state of honour I am
    perfect. 65
I doubt some danger does approach you
    nearly:
If you will take a homely man's advice,
Be not found here; hence, with your little
    ones.
To fright you thus, methinks I am too savage;
To do worse to you were fell cruelty, 70
Which is too nigh your person. Heaven
    preserve you!
I dare abide no longer. *(Exit.)*
L. MACD. Whither should I fly?
I have done no harm. But I remember now
I am in this earthly world, where to do harm
Is often laudable, to do good sometime 75
Accounted dangerous folly: why then, alas,
Do I put up that womanly defence,
To say I have done no harm?—What are
    these faces?

(Enter Murderers.)

FIRST MUR. Where is your husband?
L. MACD. I hope, in no place so unsanctified
80
Where such as thou mayst find him.
FIRST MUR. He's a traitor.
SON. Thou liest, thou shag-ear'd villain!
FIRST MUR. What, you egg!

(Stabbing him.)

Young fry of treachery!
SON. He has kill'd me, mother:

Run away, I pray you! *(Dies.)*

(Exit Lady Macduff, crying 'Murder!' Exeunt murderers,
following her.)

SCENE III. ENGLAND. BEFORE THE KING'S PALACE

(Enter Malcolm and Macduff.)

MAL. Let us seek out some desolate shade,
    and there
Weep our sad bosoms empty.
MACD. Let us rather
Hold fast the mortal sword, and like
    good men
Bestride our down-fall'n birthdom: each
    new morn
New widows howl, new orphans cry, new
    sorrows 5
Strike heaven on the face, that it resounds
As if it felt with Scotland and yell'd out
Like syllable of dolour.
MAL. What I believe, I'll wail;
What know, believe; and what I can redress,
As I shall find the time to friend, I will. 10
What you have spoke, it may be so perchance.
This tyrant, whose sole name blisters our
    tongues,
Was once thought honest: you have loved him
    well;
He hath not touch'd you yet. I am young; but
    something
You may deserve of him through me; and
    wisdom 15
To offer up a weak, poor, innocent lamb
To appease an angry god.

MACD. I am not treacherous.

MAL. But Macbeth is.

A good and virtuous nature may recoil

In an imperial charge. But I shall crave your
pardon; 20

That which you are, my thoughts cannot
transpose:

Angels are bright still, though the brightest
fell:

Though all things foul would wear the brows
of grace,

Yet grace must still look so.

MACD. I have lost my hopes.

MAL. Perchance even there where I did find
my doubts. 25

Why in that rawness left you wife and child,

Those precious motives, those strong knots of
love,

Without leave-taking? I pray you,

Let not my jealousies be your dishonours,

But mine own safeties. You may be rightly
just, 30

Whatever I shall think.

MACD. Bleed, bleed, poor country:

Great tyranny, lay thou thy basis sure,

For goodness dare not check thee: wear thou
thy wrongs;

The title is affeer'd. Fare thee well, lord:

I would not be the villain that thou think'st 35

For the whole space that's in the tyrant's
grasp

And the rich East to boot.

MAL. Be not offended:

I speak not as in absolute fear of you.

I think our country sinks beneath the yoke;

It weeps, it bleeds, and each new day a gash 40

Is added to her wounds: I think withal

There would be hands uplifted in my right;
And here from gracious England have I offer
Of goodly thousands: but for all this,
When I shall tread upon the tyrant's head, 45
Or wear it on my sword, yet my poor country
Shall have more vices than it had before,
More suffer and more sundry ways than ever,
By him that shall succeed.
MACD. What should he be?
MAL. It is myself I mean: in whom I know 50
All the particulars of vice so grafted
That, when they shall be open'd, black
    Macbeth
Will seem as pure as snow, and the poor state
Esteem him as a lamb, being compared
With my confineless harms.
MACD. Not in the legions 55
Of horrid hell can come a devil more damn'd
In evils to top Macbeth.
MAL. I grant him bloody,
Luxurious, avaricious, false, deceitful,
Sudden, malicious, smacking of every sin
That has a name: but there's no bottom,
    none, 60
In my voluptuousness: your wives, your
    daughters,
Your matrons and your maids, could not
    fill up
The cistern of my lust, and my desire
All continent impediments would o'erbear,
That did oppose my will: better Macbeth 65
Than such an one to reign.
MACD. Boundless intemperance
In nature is a tyranny; it hath been
The untimely emptying of the happy throne,
And fall of many kings. But fear not yet
To take upon you what is yours: you may 70

Convey your pleasures in a spacious plenty,
And yet seem cold, the time you may so
    hoodwink:
We have willing dames enough; there
    cannot be
That vulture in you, to devour so many
As will to greatness dedicate themselves, 75
Finding it so inclined.
MAL. With this there grows
In my most ill-composed affection such
A stanchless avarice that, were I king,
I should cut off the nobles for their lands,
Desire his jewels and this other's house: 80
And my more-having would be as a sauce
To make me hunger more, that I should forge
Quarrels unjust against the good and loyal,
Destroying them for wealth.
MACD. This avarice
Sticks deeper, grows with more pernicious
    root 85
Than summer-seeming lust, and it hath been
The sword of our slain kings: yet do not fear;
Scotland hath foisons to fill up your will
Of your mere own: all these are portable,
With other graces weigh'd. 90
MAL. But I have none: the king-becoming
    graces,
As justice, verity, temperance, stableness,
Bounty, perseverance, mercy, lowliness,
Devotion, patience, courage, fortitude,
I have no relish of them, but abound 95
In the division of each several crime,
Acting it many ways. Nay, had I power, I
    should
Pour the sweet milk of concord into hell,
Uproar the universal peace, confound
All unity on earth.

MACD. O Scotland, Scotland! 100

MAL. If such a one be fit to govern, speak:
I am as I have spoken.

MACD. Fit to govern!
No, not to live. O nation miserable!
With an untitled tyrant bloody-scepter'd,
When shalt thou see thy wholesome days
    again, 105
Since that the truest issue of thy throne
By his own interdiction stands accursed,
And does blaspheme his breed? Thy royal
    father
Was a most sainted king: the queen that bore
    thee,
Oftener upon her knees than on her feet, 110
Died every day she lived. Fare thee well!
These evils thou repeat'st upon thyself
Have banish'd me from Scotland. O my
    breast,
Thy hope ends here!

MAL. Macduff, this noble passion,
Child of integrity, hath from my soul 115
Wiped the black scruples, reconciled my
    thoughts
To thy good truth and honour. Devilish
    Macbeth
By many of these trains hath sought to
    win me
Into his power; and modest wisdom
    plucks me
From over-credulous haste: but God above 120
Deal between thee and me! for even now
I put myself to thy direction, and
Unspeak mine own detraction; here abjure
The taints and blames I laid upon myself,
For strangers to my nature. I am yet 125
Unknown to woman, never was forsworn,

Scarcely have coveted what was mine own,
At no time broke my faith, would not betray
The devil to his fellow, and delight
No less in truth than life: my first false
    speaking 130
Was this upon myself: what I am truly,
Is thine and my poor country's to command:
Whither indeed, before thy here-approach,
Old Siward, with ten thousand warlike men,
Already at a point, was setting forth. 135
Now we'll together, and the chance of
    goodness
Be like our warranted quarrel! Why are you
    silent?

MACD. Such welcome and unwelcome things
    at once
'Tis hard to reconcile.

(Enter a Doctor.)

MAL. Well, more anon. Comes the king
    forth, I pray you?140
DOCT. Ay, sir; there are a crew of wretched
    souls
That stay his cure: their malady convinces
The great assay of art; but at his touch,
Such sanctity hath heaven given his hand,
They presently amend.
MAL. I thank you, doctor. *(Exit Doctor.)*145
MACD. What's the disease he means?
MAL. 'Tis call'd the evil:
A most miraculous work in this good king;
Which often, since my here-remain in
    England,
I have seen him do. How he solicits heaven,
Himself best knows: but strangely-visited
    people, 150

All swoln and ulcerous, pitiful to the eye,
The mere despair of surgery, he cures,
Hanging a golden stamp about their necks,
Put on with holy prayers: and 'tis spoken,
To the succeeding royalty he leaves 155
The healing benediction. With this strange
    virtue
He hath a heavenly gift of prophecy,
And sundry blessings hang about his throne
That speak him full of grace.
(Enter Ross.)
Macd. See, who comes here?
Mal. My countryman; but yet I know him
    not. 160
Macd. My ever gentle cousin, welcome
    hither.
Mal. I know him now: good God, betimes
    remove
The means that makes us strangers!
Ross. Sir, amen.
Macd. Stands Scotland where it did?
Ross. Alas, poor country!
Almost afraid to know itself! It cannot 165
Be call'd our mother, but our grave: where
    nothing,
But who knows nothing, is once seen to smile;
Where sighs and groans and shrieks that rend
    the air,
Are made, not mark'd; where violent sorrow
    seems
A modern ecstasy: the dead man's knell 170
Is there scarce ask'd for who; and good men's
    lives
Expire before the flowers in their caps,
Dying or ere they sicken.
Macd. O, relation
Too nice, and yet too true!

MAL. What's the newest grief?

ROSS. That of an hour's age doth hiss the
    speaker; 175
Each minute teems a new one.

MACD. How does my wife?

ROSS. Why, well.

MACD. And all my children?

ROSS. Well too.

MACD. The tyrant has not batter'd at their
    peace?

ROSS. No; they were well at peace when I did
    leave 'em.

MACD. Be not a niggard of your speech: how
    goes 't? 180

ROSS. When I came hither to transport the
    tidings,
Which I have heavily borne, there ran a
    rumour
Of many worthy fellows that were out;
Which was to my belief witness'd the rather,
For that I saw the tyrant's power a-foot: 185
Now is the time of help; your eye in Scotland
Would create soldiers, make our women fight,
To doff their dire distresses.

MAL. Be't their comfort
We are coming thither: gracious England
    hath
Lent us good Siward and ten thousand
    men; 190
An older and a better soldier none
That Christendom gives out.

ROSS. Would I could answer
This comfort with the like! But I have words
That would be howl'd out in the desert air,
Where hearing should not latch them.

MACD. What concern they? 195
The general cause? or is it a fee-grief

Due to some single breast?

Ross. No mind that's honest
But in it shares some woe, though the
   main part
Pertains to you alone.

Macd. If it be mine,
Keep it not from me, quickly let me have
   it. 200

Ross. Let not your ears despise my tongue
   for ever,
Which shall possess them with the heaviest
   sound
That ever yet they heard.

Macd. Hum! I guess at it.

Ross. Your castle is surprised; your wife and
   babes
Savagely slaughter'd: to relate the manner, 205
Were, on the quarry of these murder'd deer,
To add the death of you.

Mal. Merciful heaven!
What, man! ne'er pull your hat upon your
   brows;
Give sorrow words: the grief that does not
   speak
Whispers the o'er-fraught heart, and bids it
   break. 210

Macd. My children too?

Ross. Wife, children, servants, all
That could be found.

Macd. And I must be from thence!
My wife kill'd too?

Ross. I have said.

Mal. Be comforted:
Let's make us medicines of our great revenge,
To cure this deadly grief. 215

Macd. He has no children. All my pretty
   ones?

Did you say all? O hell-kite! All?
What, all my pretty chickens and their dam
At one fell swoop?
MAL. Dispute it like a man.
MACD. I shall do so; 220
But I must also feel it as a man:
I cannot but remember such things were,
That were most precious to me. Did heaven
    look on,
And would not take their part? Sinful
    Macduff,
They were all struck for thee! naught that I
    am, 225
Not for their own demerits, but for mine,
Fell slaughter on their souls: heaven rest
    them now!
MAL. Be this the whetstone of your sword:
    let grief
Convert to anger; blunt not the heart,
    enrage it.
MACD. O, I could play the woman with mine
    eyes, 230
And braggart with my tongue! But, gentle
    heavens,
Cut short all intermission; front to front
Bring thou this fiend of Scotland and myself;
Within my sword's length set him; if he
    'scape,
Heaven forgive him too!
MAL. This tune goes manly. 235
Come, go we to the king; our power is ready;
Our lack is nothing but our leave. Macbeth
Is ripe for shaking, and the powers above
Put on their instruments. Receive what cheer
    you may;
The night is long that never finds the day.
    (Exeunt.) 240

ACT V.

SCENE I. DUNSINANE. ANTE-ROOM IN THE CASTLE.

(Enter a Doctor of Physic and a Waiting-Gentlewoman.)

DOCT. I have two nights watched with you, but can perceive
no truth in your report. When was it she last walked?

GENT. Since his majesty went into the field, I have seen
her rise from her bed, throw her nightgown upon her, unlock
her closet, take forth paper, fold it, write upon't, read it, ₅
afterwards seal it, and again return to bed; yet all this
while in a most fast sleep.

DOCT. A great perturbation in nature, to receive at once
the benefit of sleep and do the effects of watching! In this

87

slumbery agitation, besides her walking and
other actual ₁₀
performances, what, at any time, have you
heard her say?

GENT. That, sir, which I will not report
after her.

DOCT. You may to me, and 'tis most meet
you should.

GENT. Neither to you nor any one, having no
witness
to confirm my speech.

(Enter Lady Macbeth, with a taper.)

Lo you, here she comes! ₁₅
This is her very guise, and, upon my life, fast
asleep. Observe
her; stand close.

DOCT. How came she by that light?

GENT. Why, it stood by her: she has light by
her continually;
'tis her command. ₂₀

DOCT. You see, her eyes are open.

GENT. Ay, but their sense is shut.

DOCT. What is it she does now? Look, how
she rubs
her hands.

GENT. It is an accustomed action with her, to
seem thus ₂₅
washing her hands: I have known her
continue in this a
quarter of an hour.

LADY M. Yet here's a spot.

DOCT. Hark! she speaks: I will set down what
comes
from her, to satisfy my remembrance the
more strongly. ₃₀

LADY M. Out, damned spot! out, I say!
  One: two:
why, then 'tis time to do't. Hell is murky. Fie,
  my lord,
fie! a soldier, and afeard? What need we fear
  who knows
it, when none can call our power to account? Yet who
would have thought the old man to have had
  so much 35
blood in him?

DOCT. Do you mark that?

LADY M. The thane of Fife had a wife;
  where is she
now? What, will these hands ne'er be clean?
  No more
o' that, my lord, no more o' that: you mar all
  with this 40
starting.

DOCT. Go to, go to; you have known what
  you should
not.

GENT. She has spoke what she should not, I
  am sure of
that: heaven knows what she has known. 45

LADY M. Here's the smell of the blood still:
  all the
perfumes of Arabia will not sweeten this little
  hand. Oh,
oh, oh!

DOCT. What a sigh is there! The heart is
  sorely charged.

GENT. I would not have such a heart in my
  bosom for 50
the dignity of the whole body.

DOCT. Well, well, well,—

GENT. Pray God it be, sir.

DOCT. This disease is beyond my practice:
    yet I have
known those which have walked in their sleep
    who have ₅₅
died holily in their beds.
LADY M. Wash your hands; put on your
    nightgown;
look not so pale: I tell you yet again, Banquo's
    buried;
he cannot come out on 's grave.
DOCT. Even so? ₆₀
LADY M. To bed, to bed; there's knocking at
    the gate:
come, come, come, come, give me your hand:
    what's done
cannot be undone: to bed, to bed, to bed.
    (Exit.)
DOCT. Will she go now to bed?
GENT. Directly. ₆₅
DOCT. Foul whisperings are abroad:
    unnatural deeds
Do breed unnatural troubles: infected minds
To their deaf pillows will discharge their
    secrets:
More needs she the divine than the physician.
God, God forgive us all! Look after her; ₇₀
Remove from her the means of all
    annoyance,
And still keep eyes upon her. So good night:
My mind she has mated and amazed my
    sight:
I think, but dare not speak.
GENT. Good night, good doctor.

(Exeunt.)

SCENE II. THE COUNTRY NEAR DUNSINANE

(Drum and colours. Enter Menteith, Caithness, Angus, Lennox, and Soldiers.)

MENT. The English power is near, led on by Malcolm,
His uncle Siward and the good Macduff:
Revenges burn in them; for their dear causes
Would to the bleeding and the grim alarm
Excite the mortified man.
ANG. Near Birnam wood 5
Shall we well meet them; that way are they coming.
CAITH. Who knows if Donalbain be with his brother?
LEN. For certain, sir, he is not: I have a file
Of all the gentry: there is Siward's son,
And many unrough youths, that even now 10
Protest their first of manhood.
MENT. What does the tyrant?
CAITH. Great Dunsinane he strongly fortifies:
Some say he's mad; others, that lesser hate him,
Do call it valiant fury: but, for certain,
He cannot buckle his distemper'd cause 15
Within the belt of rule.
ANG. Now does he feel
His secret murders sticking on his hands;
Now minutely revolts upbraid his faith-breach;
Those he commands move only in command,
Nothing in love: now does he feel his title 20
Hang loose about him, like a giant's robe
Upon a dwarfish thief.
MENT. Who then shall blame

His pester'd senses to recoil and start,
When all that is within him does condemn
Itself for being there?
CAITH. Well, march we on, 25
To give obedience where 'tis truly owed:
Meet we the medicine of the sickly weal,
And with him pour we, in our country's
    purge,
Each drop of us.
LEN. Or so much as it needs
To dew the sovereign flower and drown the
    weeds. 30
Make we our march towards Birnam. *(Exeunt,*
    marching.)

SCENE III. DUSINANE. A ROOM IN THE CASTLE.

(Enter Macbeth, Doctor, and Attendants.)

MACB. Bring me no more reports; let them
    fly all:
Till Birnam wood remove to Dunsinane
I cannot taint with fear. What's the boy
    Malcolm?
Was he not born of woman? The spirits
    that know
All mortal consequences have pronounced
    me thus: 5
'Fear not, Macbeth; no man that's born of
    woman
Shall e'er have power upon thee.' Then fly,
    false thanes,
And mingle with the English epicures:
The mind I sway by and the heart I bear
Shall never sag with doubt nor shake with
    fear. 10

(Enter a Servant.)

The devil damn thee black, thou cream-faced
    loon!
Where got'st thou that goose look?
SERV. There is ten thousand—
MACB. Geese, villain?
SERV. Soldiers, sir.
MACB. Go prick thy face and over-red thy
    fear,
Thou lily-liver'd boy. What soldiers, patch? 15
Death of thy soul! those linen cheeks of thine
Are counsellors to fear. What soldiers, whey-
    face?
SERV. The English force, so please you.
MACB. Take thy face hence. *(Exit Servant.)*
Seyton!—I am sick at heart,
When I behold—Seyton, I say!—This push 20
Will cheer me ever, or disseat me now.
I have lived long enough: my way of life
Is fall'n into the sear, the yellow leaf,
And that which should accompany old age,
As honour, love, obedience, troops of
    friends, 25
I must not look to have; but, in their stead,
Curses, not loud but deep, mouth-honour,
    breath,
Which the poor heart would fain deny, and
    dare not.
Seyton!

(Enter Seyton.)

SEY. What's your gracious pleasure?
MACB. What news more? 30
SEY. All is confirmed, my lord, which was
    reported.

MACB. I'll fight, till from my bones my flesh
    be hack'd.

Give me my armour.

SEY. 'Tis not needed yet.

MACB. I'll put it on.

Send out moe horses, skirr the country
    round; 35

Hang those that talk of fear. Give me mine
    armour.

How does your patient, doctor?

DOCT. Not so sick, my lord,

As she is troubled with thick-coming fancies,

That keep her from her rest.

MACB. Cure her of that.

Canst thou not minister to a mind diseased, 40

Pluck from the memory a rooted sorrow,

Raze out the written troubles of the brain,

And with some sweet oblivious antidote

Cleanse the stuff'd bosom of that perilous
    stuff

Which weighs upon the heart?

DOCT. Therein the patient 45

Must minister to himself.

MACB. Throw physic to the dogs, I'll none
    of it.

Come, put mine armour on; give me my
    staff.

Seyton, send out. Doctor, the thanes fly
    from me.

Come, sir, dispatch. If thou couldst, doctor,
    cast 50

The water of my land, find her disease

And purge it to a sound and pristine health,

I would applaud thee to the very echo,

That should applaud again. Pull't off, I say.

What rhubarb, cyme, or what purgative
    drug, 55

Would scour these English hence? Hear'st
    thou of them?

Doct. Ay, my good lord; your royal
    preparation

Makes us hear something.

Macb. Bring it after me.

I will not be afraid of death and bane

Till Birnam forest come to Dunsinane. 60

Doct. *(Aside)* Were I from Dunsinane away
    and clear,

Profit again should hardly draw me here.

(Exeunt.)

SCENE IV. COUNTRY NEAR BIRNAM WOOD

(Drum and colours. Enter Malcolm, old Siward and his Son, Macduff, Menteith, Caithness, Angus, Lennox, Ross, and Soldiers, marching.)

Mal. Cousins, I hope the days are near
    at hand

That chambers will be safe.

Ment. We doubt it nothing.

Siw. What wood is this before us?

Ment. The wood of Birnam.

Mal. Let every soldier hew him down a
    bough,

And bear't before him: thereby shall we
    shadow 5

The numbers of our host, and make
    discovery

Err in report of us.

Soldiers. It shall be done.

Siw. We learn no other but the confident
    tyrant

Keeps still in Dunsinane, and will endure
Our setting down before 't.
MAL. 'Tis his main hope: $_{10}$
For where there is advantage to be given,
Both more and less have given him the revolt,
And none serve with him but constrained
    things
Whose hearts are absent too.
MACD. Let our just censures
Attend the true event, and put we on $_{15}$
Industrious soldiership.
SIW. The time approaches,
That will with due decision make us know
What we shall say we have and what we owe.
Thoughts speculative their unsure hopes
    relate,
But certain issue strokes must arbitrate: $_{20}$
Towards which advance the war. *(Exeunt,
    marching.)*

SCENE V. DUNSINANE. WITHIN THE CASTLE

(Enter Macbeth, Seyton, and Soldiers, with drum and colours.)

    MACB. Hang out our banners on the
        outward walls;
The cry is still 'They come:' our castle's
    strength
Will laugh a siege to scorn: here let them lie
Till famine and the ague eat them up:
Were they not forced with those that should
    be ours, $_5$
We might have met them dareful, beard to
    beard,
And beat them backward home. *(A cry of
    women within.)*

What is that noise?

SEY. It is the cry of women, my good lord.
  (Exit.)

MACB. I have almost forgot the taste of
  fears:

The time has been, my senses would have
  cool'd 10

To hear a night-shriek, and my fell of hair

Would at a dismal treatise rouse and stir

As life were in 't: I have supp'd full with
  horrors;

Direness, familiar to my slaughterous
  thoughts,

Cannot once start me.

(Re-enter Seyton.)

Wherefore was that cry? 15

SEY. The queen, my lord, is dead.

MACB. She should have died hereafter;

There would have been a time for such a
  word.

To-morrow, and to-morrow, and to-morrow,

Creeps in this petty pace from day to day, 20

To the last syllable of recorded time;

And all our yesterdays have lighted fools

The way to dusty death. Out, out, brief
  candle!

Life's but a walking shadow, a poor player

That struts and frets his hour upon the
  stage 25

And then is heard no more: it is a tale

Told by an idiot, full of sound and fury,

Signifying nothing.

(Enter a Messenger.)

Thou comest to use thy tongue; thy story
    quickly.
MESS. Gracious my lord, 30
I should report that which I say I saw,
But know not how to do it.
MACB. Well, say, sir.
MESS. As I did stand my watch upon the hill,
I look'd toward Birnam, and anon,
    methought,
The wood began to move.
MACB. Liar and slave! 35
MESS. Let me endure your wrath, if't be
    not so:
Within this three mile may you see it coming;
I say, a moving grove.
MACB. If thou speak'st false,
Upon the next tree shalt thou hang alive,
Till famine cling thee: if thy speech be
    sooth, 40
I care not if thou dost for me as much.
I pull in resolution, and begin
To doubt the equivocation of the fiend
That lies like truth: 'Fear not, till
    Birnam wood
Do come to Dunsinane;' and now a wood 45
Comes toward Dunsinane. Arm, arm,
    and out!
If this which he avouches does appear,
There is nor flying hence nor tarrying here.
I 'gin to be a-weary of the sun,
And wish the estate o' the world were now
    undone. 50
Ring the alarum-bell! Blow, wind! come,
    wrack!
At least we'll die with harness on our back.

(Exeunt.)

SCENE VI. DUNSINANE. BEFORE THE CASTLE

(Drum and colours. Enter Malcolm, old Siward, Macduff, and their Army, with boughs.)

MAL. Now near enough; your leavy screens throw down,
And show like those you are. You, worthy uncle,
Shall, with my cousin, your right noble son,
Lead our first battle: worthy Macduff and we
Shall take upon 's what else remains to do, 5
According to our order.
SIW. Fare you well.
Do we but find the tyrant's power to-night,
Let us be beaten, if we cannot fight.
MACD. Make all our trumpets speak; give them all breath,
Those clamorous harbingers of blood and death. *(Exeunt.)* 10

SCENE VII. ANOTHER PART OF THE FIELD

(Alarums. Enter Macbeth.)

MACB. They have tied me to a stake; I cannot fly,
But bear-like I must fight the course. What's he
That was not born of woman? Such a one
Am I to fear, or none.

(Enter young Siward.)

YO. SIW. What is thy name?

MACB. Thou'lt be afraid to hear it.

YO. SIW. No; though thou call'st thyself a hotter name
Than any is in hell.

MACB. My name 's Macbeth.

YO. SIW. The devil himself could not pronounce a title
More hateful to mine ear.

MACB. No, nor more fearful.

YO. SIW. Thou liest, abhorred tyrant; with my sword 10
I'll prove the lie thou speak'st.

(They fight, and young Siward is slain.)

MACB. Thou wast born of woman.
But swords I smile at, weapons laugh to scorn,
Brandish'd by man that's of a woman born.
(Exit.)

(Alarums. Enter Macduff.)

MACD. That way the noise is. Tyrant, show thy face!
If thou be'st slain and with no stroke of mine, 15
My wife and children's ghosts will haunt me still.
I cannot strike at wretched kerns, whose arms
Are hired to bear their staves: either thou, Macbeth,
Or else my sword, with an unbatter'd edge,
I sheathe again undeeded. There thou shouldst be; 20
By this great clatter, one of greatest note
Seems bruited: let me find him, fortune!

And more I beg not. *(Exit. Alarums.)*

(Enter Malcolm and old Siward.)

SIW. This way, my lord; the castle's gently
    render'd:
The tyrant's people on both sides do fight; 25
The noble thanes do bravely in the war;
The day almost itself professes yours,
And little is to do.
MAL. We have met with foes
That strike beside us.
SIW. Enter, sir, the castle.

(Exeunt. Alarum.)

SCENE VIII. ANOTHER PART OF THE FIELD

(Enter Macbeth.)

MACB. Why should I play the Roman fool,
    and die
On mine own sword? whiles I see lives, the
    gashes
Do better upon them.

(Enter Macduff.)

MACD. Turn, hell-hound, turn!
MACB. Of all men else I have avoided thee:
But get thee back; my soul is too much
    charged 5
With blood of thine already.
MACD. I have no words:
My voice is in my sword, thou bloodier villain
Than terms can give thee out! *(They fight.)*

MACB. Thou losest labour:
As easy mayst thou the intrenchant air
With thy keen sword impress as make me
    bleed: 10
Let fall thy blade on vulnerable crests;
I bear a charmed life, which must not yield
To one of woman born.
MACD. Despair thy charm,
And let the angel whom thou still hast served
Tell thee, Macduff was from his mother's
    womb 15
Untimely ripp'd.
MACB. Accursed be that tongue that tells
    me so,
For it hath cow'd my better part of man!
And be these juggling fiends no more
    believed,
That palter with us in a double sense; 20
That keep the word of promise to our ear,
And break it to our hope. I 'll not fight with
    thee.
MACD. Then yield thee, coward,
And live to be the show and gaze o' the time:
We'll have thee, as our rarer monsters are, 25
Painted upon a pole, and underwrit,
'Here may you see the tyrant.'
MACB. I will not yield,
To kiss the ground before young Malcolm's
    feet,
And to be baited with the rabble's curse.
Though Birnam wood be come to
    Dunsinane, 30
And thou opposed, being of no woman born,
Yet I will try the last: before my body
I throw my warlike shield: lay on, Macduff;
And damn'd be him that first cries 'Hold,
    enough!'

(Exeunt, fighting. Alarums.)

(Retreat. Flourish. Enter, with drum and colours, Malcolm, old Siward, Ross, the other Thanes, and Soldiers.)

MAL. I would the friends we miss were safe
    arrived. 35
SIW. Some must go off: and yet, by these
    I see,
So great a day as this is cheaply bought.
MAL. Macduff is missing, and your
    noble son.
ROSS. Your son, my lord, has paid a soldier's
    debt:
He only lived but till he was a man; 40
The which no sooner had his prowess
    confirm'd
In the unshrinking station where he fought,
But like a man he died.
SIW. Then he is dead?
ROSS. Ay, and brought off the field: your
    cause of sorrow
Must not be measured by his worth, for
    then 45
It hath no end.
SIW. Had he his hurts before?
ROSS. Ay, on the front.
SIW. Why then, God's soldier be he!
Had I as many sons as I have hairs,
I would not wish them to a fairer death:
And so his knell is knoll'd.
MAL. He's worth more sorrow, 50
And that I'll spend for him.
SIW. He's worth no more:
They say he parted well and paid his score:
And so God be with him! Here comes newer
    comfort.

(Re-enter Macduff, with Macbeth's head.)

MACD. Hail, king! for so thou art: behold,
    where stands
The usurper's cursed head: the time is free: 55
I see thee compass'd with thy kingdom's
    pearl,
That speak my salutation in their minds;
Whose voices I desire aloud with mine:
Hail, King of Scotland!
ALL. Hail, King of Scotland! *(Flourish.)*
MAL. We shall not spend a large expense of
    time 60
Before we reckon with your several loves,
And make us even with you. My thanes and
    kinsmen,
Henceforth be earls, the first that ever
    Scotland
In such an honour named. What's more
    to do,
Which would be planted newly with the
    time, 65
As calling home our exiled friends abroad
That fled the snares of watchful tyranny,
Producing forth the cruel ministers
Of this dead butcher and his fiend-like
    queen,
Who, as 'tis thought, by self and violent
    hands 70
Took off her life; this, and what needful else
That calls upon us, by the grace of Grace
We will perform in measure, time and place:
So thanks to all at once and to each one,
Whom we invite to see us crown'd at
    Scone. 75

(Flourish. Exeunt.)

Made in the USA
Monee, IL
07 April 2022

94289971R00069